HOAXSTERS, Inc.

*How The Left Pushes False Narratives To
Promote Division In America*

Written by Paul King

TABLE OF CONTENTS

TEXAS BORDER PATROL WHIPPING ILLEGAL
MIGRANTS ENTERING AMERICA

****** RACE BAITING FRAUDS******

JUSSIE SMOLLETT

BUBBA WALLACE

"HANDS UP, DON'T SHOOT"

YASMIN SEWEID BREAKS CURFEW

THE RACIST AIR FORCE

"NOT ANOTHER RACIST NOTE!?"

"TAWANA?" "NO!"

****** MEDIA NARRATIVES TO DIVIDE ******

THE COVINGTON KIDS

THE RITTENHOUSE AFFAIR

DUKE LACROSSE R*PE

MICHIGAN KIDNAPPING

"WE'RE COMING FOR KAVANAUGH NOW"

"BUT FIRST WE HAVE TO GET THOMAS"

"WOKE" IS A HOAX

FOREWORD

Shortly after the events on January 6th, 2021 a distant cousin reached out via Facebook DM to talk. Though we are 'friends' on the platform, I call him "distant" for several reasons:

1. We rarely talk.
2. I haven't seen him in over a decade.
3. I have no idea what his life is like.
4. He lives in California and I live in Florida.

The conversation started genial enough with the obligatory, "Hey, how are you?", but it wasn't long before he was asking offbeat questions, left leaning in nature, and I began feeling like I was being set up in a trap.

To be clear, I went to stay with his family 30 years before this and even then they were heavily involved in the law enforcement community, otherwise known as law enforcement organizations (LEOs for short).

On Facebook and other pages I've been a vocal supporter of Donald Trump. And yes, I did vote for him both times. And also yes, I think he was robbed in the 2020 debacle and sham of an 'election' where even Biden himself said on camera "we built the largest election fraud network" (did they ever!).

That said, it doesn't happen often that I talk politics with someone in real life. Typically I only talk to a person based on our mutual connection to any certain topic, "oh you like music? Me too.", "You're into playing Starcraft? That's cool, I used to be."

Occasionally I will talk about politics - if that's what we have in common. My cousin had to have known that I was a Christian, a conservative, and MAGA supporter and maybe in his mind that's what we had in common. Except ...

This cousin of mine, seeing the events unfold on January 6th, wondered if I wanted to be in law enforcement of some type. Um, no.?

But he pressed forward, "The truth is on Jan 6th there was an attempted coup in this great country of ours!" (essentially, ostensibly) ... Good grief.

I quickly changed the subject. Not desiring to get entrapped into saying something that could be used against me, all while causing a disagreement, is one of my 'better traits'. Life is too short.

Did he want me to 'infiltrate' "my kind"? Was he wondering if I truly had an interest in LEOs? I'll never know because I'll never ask.

The next time I heard from him, my favorite aunt, his mother, had passed away.

I hadn't recalled our conversation in some years until I saw a meme being posted around the Twitter / X space which listed many of the things we now know, for a fact, are hoaxes – with much of January 6th being one of the biggest.

And hoaxes are what we're going to talk about in this book. Why? Because some people are still under the spell of whatever lies they've been told to believe, and so, they willfully do because it fits their own personal narrative and what they hope to "achieve" with their life.

And keep in mind, to those who haven't been 'red pilled' (as others call it) this could seem like a laundry list of conspiracy theories. Which would be the case if the initial story told wasn't completely debunked by facts. And by facts I'm not talking about 'fact checkers'; those snot nosed 22 year olds fresh out of college indoctrination camps eager to share their knowledge with the rest of the world in the hope that finally, once and for all, they may have power and bring some meaning in their lives. I mean, the actual truth. The 'real', as the Matrix would put it.

Buckle up.

RUSSIA RUSSIA RUSSIA!

Perhaps the first thing that got me thinking about all these hoaxes in the media happening (besides a healthy belief there's no way in the world we ever had men on the moon!) was this "Russia, Russia, Russia!" stuff Hillary cooked up in her demented basement with a bunch of nefarious characters - also known as "government employees", with security clearance.

To be fair, it could have been true, but … no, no, it couldn't.

Admittedly, I've been a fan of Trump since I was 14 years old and The Art of the Deal came out. By that time I was already reading the Forbes 400 and watching "Lifestyles of the Rich and Famous" on TV. The book was a pretty amazing look into the daily life of a real tycoon. I took 3 pages of handwritten notes from the book and my original copy (long since lost to the history bins of constant moving after the parents divorce) looked like my moms Bible – paragraphs and words underlined for emphasis.

I was the only kid in the world with the Trump board game, which I never even opened knowing that one day it would be worth something (that is lost too).

I knew at the time that Donald Trump was a special person, successful in each and every single way, for everything he set out to do. What I didn't know was that one day he would become the President of the United States.

He had always toyed with becoming President, or at least been forced to talk about it from time to time. People like Oprah Winfrey and others would ask him about it on their TV shows - even when he was much, much younger. Fast forward 30 years or so and he decided to run.

Until this time no one had ever suggested in any way, shape, form, or fashion that Donald Trump, the owner of Trump Tower and all these other properties all over the world, was a Russian spy - not until Hillary Clinton decided to do it on her own, with the help of some not so healthy people. And talk about a job! She really did one.

It's one of the biggest hoaxes in America's history, if not one of the largest ever hoaxes in the history of the world.

This is what AI has to say about it:

The term "Russian collusion" refers to allegations that

Donald Trump's campaign conspired or coordinated with Russia to influence the 2016 U.S. presidential election. The controversy spanned several years, involving extensive investigations, media coverage, and political debate.

Origins and Campaign Allegations

The origins of the Russian collusion narrative date back to the 2016 presidential campaign. As early as 2015, U.S. intelligence agencies observed suspicious activities suggesting Russian attempts to interfere in the electoral process. The situation intensified in June 2016 when the Democratic National Committee (DNC) announced that its servers had been hacked by Russian operatives.

In July 2016, WikiLeaks began releasing thousands of emails from the DNC, leading to accusations that the Trump campaign might be cooperating with Russia. Trump's public praise of Russian President Vladimir Putin and his encouragement of Russia to find Hillary Clinton's missing emails fueled speculation.

Investigation and Key Events

The formal investigation began in July 2016, led by the FBI, focusing on links between Trump associates and Russian officials. After Trump's victory and subsequent inauguration, the investigation's scope widened, eventually leading to the appointment of Robert Mueller as Special

Counsel in May 2017.

Mueller's investigation aimed to determine whether the Trump campaign colluded with Russia and whether there was any obstruction of justice by Trump or his associates. Over the next two years, the investigation led to indictments, convictions, or plea deals for several Trump associates, though these were often for matters not directly related to Russian collusion, such as financial crimes and lying to investigators.

Media and Public Perception

Throughout the investigation, the media played a significant role in shaping public perception. Many news outlets reported extensively on the potential collusion, with some suggesting that the evidence was strong enough to warrant impeachment. In contrast, conservative media outlets often criticized the investigation as a "witch hunt" and questioned the integrity of the investigators.

The Mueller Report and Its Aftermath

The pivotal moment came in April 2019 when Mueller's report was released. The report concluded that there was insufficient evidence to establish that Trump or his campaign conspired with Russia to influence the 2016 election. However, it did not exonerate Trump on obstruction of justice, instead detailing several instances where his actions could be interpreted as such, leaving the decision to Congress.

The release of the report did not end the debate. Democrats argued that the report contained evidence of misconduct, while Republicans claimed it exonerated Trump completely. The phrase "no collusion" became a rallying cry for Trump and his supporters.

Controversies and Criticisms

The investigation and its coverage have been subjects of controversy. Critics argued that the investigation was politically motivated, citing concerns about the origins of the FBI's investigation, including the role of the Steele dossier, a collection of intelligence reports that contained unverified allegations about Trump's ties to Russia.

In the following years, reviews and investigations into the origins of the Russia probe, including the Department of Justice's Inspector General report, criticized aspects of the FBI's actions, such as errors and omissions in surveillance applications. However, these reviews did not substantiate claims that the investigation was a complete "hoax" or entirely unjustified.

Conclusion

The narrative of Russian collusion and the subsequent

investigation were complex and polarizing, reflecting broader political and social divisions. While the Mueller report did not find conclusive evidence of collusion, it also highlighted Russian interference in the election and raised questions about the conduct of various individuals involved in the Trump campaign.

The term "hoax," as used by some to describe the Russian collusion narrative, reflects the deep partisanship and skepticism towards the institutions involved in the investigation. It underscores how political, legal, and media dynamics can influence public understanding and trust in democratic processes. END

No, it underscores the whole thing was a hoax. Even a sensible non-partisan can see that now. And worse, this hoax continues.

HUNTER'S LAPTOP

C'mon!? You're telling me that the guys SELFIE PICTURES are all over the laptop – using drugs and using hookers – doing drugs and doing hookers – rolling drugs and rolling hookers – showing his 'junk' and showing the hookers 'junk' (for lack of a better term), and it isn't HIS?!?!

AI does it's best to help us understand what happened:

The Hunter Biden laptop story, which emerged in October 2020, weeks before the U.S. presidential election, became a focal point of controversy and debate. Initially dismissed by many as disinformation, subsequent developments have complicated the narrative, leading to ongoing discussions about media bias, censorship, and foreign interference in American politics.

The Emergence of the Laptop Story

The story began when the New York Post published a series of articles claiming that a laptop allegedly belonging to Hunter Biden, son of then-presidential candidate Joe Biden, contained emails and other materials suggesting questionable business dealings in Ukraine and China. The laptop was reportedly left at a Delaware repair shop in 2019 and never retrieved. The shop owner claimed to have provided the laptop's contents to Rudy Giuliani, former New York City Mayor and then-lawyer for President Donald Trump, who then gave it to the Post.

Initial Reactions and Claims of Disinformation

The story's release was met with skepticism by many media outlets and public figures, who questioned the authenticity of the information and the circumstances of the laptop's discovery. Shortly after the story broke, 51 former intelligence officials signed a letter suggesting that the release of the emails had "all the classic earmarks of a Russian information operation." This claim significantly influenced public perception and media coverage, leading to widespread dismissal of the story as potentially Russian disinformation intended to influence the election outcome.

Social Media Censorship and Public Debate

The controversy intensified when major social media platforms, including Twitter and Facebook, took steps to limit the spread of the New York Post's articles, citing policies against the distribution of hacked materials and misinformation. Twitter temporarily locked the New York Post's account, and Facebook reduced the story's circulation pending fact-checker review. These actions sparked a heated debate over censorship, the role of social media in public discourse, and the power these platforms wield in shaping political narratives.

Subsequent Investigations and Verifications

In the months following the election, further investigations and reporting gradually lent credibility to some aspects of the laptop story. Several media outlets independently authenticated some of the emails found on the laptop, confirming that they were, indeed, sent to or from Hunter Biden. The focus shifted from the origin and pathway of the laptop's emergence to the contents' implications, particularly regarding Hunter Biden's business activities and whether they had any connection to Joe Biden's actions as Vice President.

Legal and Political Ramifications

The laptop and its contents became part of broader investigations into Hunter Biden's tax affairs and business dealings, conducted by the Department of Justice. As of now, no evidence has been publicly confirmed to show that Joe Biden was involved in or benefited from Hunter Biden's business activities. However, the ongoing investigations keep the story in the public eye, with partisan lines often dictating the narrative's interpretation.

Media Reflection and Criticism

The handling of the Hunter Biden laptop story led to introspection and criticism within the media industry. Some commentators and media figures acknowledged that the initial dismissal of the laptop story as disinformation without thorough investigation was a misstep, reflecting broader issues in journalistic practice and the potential for bias. Critics argued that the story's suppression and the initial labeling as disinformation without concrete evidence demonstrated a need for greater transparency and neutrality in journalism and social media governance.

Impact on Public Trust

The evolution of the Hunter Biden laptop story from dismissed disinformation to a subject of legitimate investigation has had a lasting impact on public trust in media and institutions. For some, the story exemplifies a perceived double standard in how information is treated based on political alignment, contributing to increasing polarization and distrust in the media and government agencies.

Conclusion

The Hunter Biden laptop story highlights the complexities and challenges of navigating the modern information landscape, where the lines between truth, disinformation, and political interests are often blurred. The story's trajectory—from initial dismissal as a potential foreign influence operation to partial authentication and ongoing legal scrutiny—underscores the difficulties in maintaining journalistic integrity and public trust in an era of rapid information dissemination and intense political polarization. END

No. There's no 'blurring' – only media (and Biden's debate) lies. Oh, and those "50" *other people* who signed a document, which was a lie.

"KILL THE KOI!"

Of all the ways to "frame Trump" as a "bad guy", the press chose … feeding fish in Japan. You just can't make this stuff up!

According to AI, here's what happened:

The incident involving President Donald Trump and the feeding of koi fish during his visit to Japan in 2017 serves as a vivid example of how media framing and editing can shape public perception and create misleading narratives.

The Incident

In November 2017, during a diplomatic trip to Japan, President Trump participated in a traditional koi feeding ceremony alongside Japanese Prime Minister Shinzo Abe at the Akasaka Palace in Tokyo. The event was intended to symbolize friendship and cooperation between the United States and Japan.

Media Coverage and Misrepresentation

Some media outlets and social media users circulated a video clip showing President Trump purportedly overfeeding the koi by dumping his entire box of fish food into the pond, seemingly in a moment of impatience or ignorance of the ceremony's etiquette. This clip was presented in a way that contrasted Trump's actions unfavorably with those of Prime Minister Abe, suggesting that Trump had disregarded the customary, more measured approach to feeding the fish.

The Full Context

However, the full video of the event tells a different story. It shows that Prime Minister Abe was the first to empty the remainder of his fish food box into the pond, after which Trump followed suit. The edited clip that was widely shared omitted this crucial context, leading to a narrative that Trump had acted improperly and disrespectfully, while in reality, he was simply mirroring the actions of his host.

Media Criticism and Public Reaction

The selective editing and coverage of the koi feeding incident led to accusations of media bias and manipulation, with critics arguing that the incident was used to unfairly ridicule President Trump. The episode became a flash point in the ongoing debate over media credibility and the perceived treatment of Trump by the press.

The incident highlighted how easily public perception can be manipulated through selective editing and reporting, contributing to the broader discussions about trust in the media and the importance of context in journalistic practices.

Broader Implications for Media and Politics

The "Trump overfeeds koi" narrative had broader implications for the relationship between the media and political figures. It underscored the challenges of maintaining objectivity and fairness in an era of intense political polarization and rapid news cycles. The incident demonstrated how seemingly minor events could be amplified and distorted, contributing to the growing skepticism and cynicism toward the news media.

Reflections on Media Ethics and Responsibility

The koi feeding incident serves as a case study in media ethics and the responsibility of journalists to provide accurate and complete information. It raises important questions about the role of the media in shaping political narratives and the potential consequences of misrepresentation, both for individuals and for the broader public discourse.

Conclusion

The misrepresentation of the koi feeding incident during President Trump's visit to Japan illustrates the power of media framing and the impact of selective editing on public perception. While ostensibly a minor event, the episode became emblematic of concerns about media bias and the importance of context in reporting. It serves as a reminder of the need for critical media consumption and the importance of comprehensive and fair journalism in democratic societies. END

VERY FINE PEOPLE

This hoax is still being used and bantered about – even know MOST competent people know better. I have a cousin that doesn't know any better, and still believes this to this day.

AI tells the story:

The controversy surrounding President Donald Trump's "very fine people" comment following the August 2017 events in Charlottesville, Virginia, is a notable example of how public statements can become the center of intense political and media scrutiny. This incident has been widely debated, with varying interpretations of Trump's remarks and their implications.

The Charlottesville Incident

The context for Trump's remarks was a series of violent clashes in Charlottesville, initiated by a rally called "Unite the Right." The rally, organized by white supremacist groups to protest the removal of a Confederate statue, attracted a mix of neo-Nazis, white nationalists, and other far-right activists. It also drew counter-protesters opposing these groups' ideologies. The situation escalated, resulting in tragic violence, including the death of Heather Heyer, a counter-protester, who was killed when a rally attendee drove his car into a crowd.

Trump's Comments

In the aftermath, President Trump made several statements about the events. The most controversial was during a press conference on August 15, 2017, where he said there were "very fine people on both sides" of the Charlottesville clashes. This comment was seized upon by media outlets and critics who interpreted it as Trump equating the counter-protesters with the white nationalists and neo-Nazis.

However, in the same press conference, Trump also explicitly condemned the neo-Nazis and white supremacists, stating, "I'm not talking about the neo-Nazis and the white nationalists, because they should be condemned totally." This part of his remarks was often downplayed or omitted in subsequent media coverage and political discourse, leading to widespread perception that Trump had broadly labeled the far-right protesters as "fine people."

Media Interpretation and Public Reaction

The media's framing of Trump's comments played a significant role in shaping public perception. Many news outlets highlighted the "very fine people on both sides" remark without providing the full context of his condemnation of the extremist groups. This selective reporting contributed to the narrative that Trump was sympathizing with white supremacists.

The resulting backlash was swift and severe, with bipartisan condemnation from politicians, civil rights organizations, and the public. Critics accused Trump of moral equivalence and of failing to adequately denounce hate groups, while some supporters argued that his comments were being misrepresented.

Impact on Political and Social Discourse

The controversy had a lasting impact on Trump's presidency and American political discourse. It intensified debates over race relations, the rise of white nationalist sentiment, and the responsibilities of political leaders to unequivocally denounce hate groups. The incident became a touchstone in discussions of Trump's rhetoric and his administration's stance on racial issues.

Analysis and Reflection

The "fine people" controversy underscores the complexities of political communication and media interpretation. It highlights how quickly narratives can be established and how difficult they can be to alter once they take hold in the public consciousness. The incident also serves as a reminder of the critical need for precise language and clear condemnation of hate when addressing volatile and sensitive issues.

Conclusion

The narrative that emerged following Trump's comments on the Charlottesville incident illustrates the power of media framing and the importance of context in public statements. While Trump's remarks included a condemnation of white supremacists and neo-Nazis, the selective focus on his "very fine people" comment contributed to a widespread and enduring controversy. This episode reflects the broader challenges of navigating and interpreting political speech in a highly polarized and media-saturated environment. END

"NOT THE TEAR GAS!"

The incident where it was reported that then-President Donald Trump had peaceful protesters cleared with tear gas for a photo opportunity in front of St. John's Episcopal Church, near the White House, became a significant and contentious moment in U.S. political history. The event occurred on June 1, 2020, amid widespread protests over the death of George Floyd and broader issues of police brutality and racial injustice.

Background of the Incident

Protests had erupted across the United States after the death of George Floyd at the hands of Minneapolis police officers. In Washington, D.C., these protests often took place near the White House, with Lafayette Square being a primary gathering site. On June 1, law enforcement officers forcibly cleared protesters from Lafayette Square shortly before President Trump walked through the area to pose for photographs in front of St. John's Church while holding a Bible.

Initial Reports and Public Outrage

Initial media reports and commentary suggested that the protesters were peacefully assembled and were dispersed with tear gas solely to clear a path for President Trump's photo opportunity. This narrative was rapidly disseminated through various media outlets and social media platforms, leading to widespread condemnation of the action as an abuse of power and an infringement on the protesters' rights.

Contradictory Evidence and Investigations

Subsequent investigations and reports, however, presented a more complex picture. The U.S. Park Police and other officials stated that the decision to clear the area was made independently of the President's movements and was intended to establish a secure perimeter around the White House in response to episodes of violence and vandalism that had occurred in the days prior. They also clarified that while tear gas was not used, smoke canisters and pepper balls were deployed to disperse the crowd.

An investigation by the Department of the Interior's Inspector General released in June 2021 found that the clearing of Lafayette Square was planned before knowing about Trump's photo op and was conducted to allow contractors to safely install anti-scale fencing. The report indicated that the law enforcement action was not executed to facilitate the President's walk to St. John's Church.

Media Criticism and Narrative Shift

The revelations from the investigation led to criticism of the media's initial portrayal of the event. Critics argued that the media had prematurely connected the clearing of the square with Trump's photo opportunity, contributing to a misleading narrative. This criticism highlighted concerns about media bias and the rush to judgment without full context, raising questions about the reliability and objectivity of news reporting in politically charged environments.

Impact on Political Discourse

The incident and its subsequent reporting had a significant impact on political discourse in the United States. It intensified debates about law enforcement tactics during protests, the right to peaceful assembly, and the relationship between the media and political figures. For supporters of President Trump, the revised understanding of the event was seen as vindication and evidence of media bias against him. For critics, the episode remained emblematic of what they perceived as his administration's disregard for democratic norms and civil rights.

Broader Societal Reflections

The controversy surrounding the Lafayette Square clearing and Trump's photo op reflects broader societal challenges in balancing security, civil liberties, and political expression. It also illustrates the critical role of media in shaping public perception and the importance of accurate and comprehensive reporting in maintaining public trust and informed discourse.

Conclusion

The narrative that emerged around the clearing of protesters in Lafayette Square for President Trump's photo opportunity demonstrates the complexities and nuances involved in real-time reporting of political and social events. While the initial reports of the incident were later contested and partially refuted, the episode left a lasting impact on public and political dialogue, underscoring the tensions in American society and the pivotal role of the media in documenting and interpreting those moments. END

These hateful. vile, and disgusting people in the media show no shame at propagating a lie like this – because it helps them with their low class viewer. And by low class, I don't mean the poorer people in society (they actually love Trump because they love America FIRST), I mean the class of people that didn't have enough classes in school to know they're being schooled by the talking heads on the TV, or those that just have "no class".

COVID-19 ORIGIN STORY

The first hoax of COVID was the Wuhan lab leak hoax. The left literally shut down any talk that this SARSv2 virus could have been created in the lab in the first place, when in fact, most logical individuals pretty much assumed it had been from the beginning. Where else could it have come from?

Oh that's right, those dirty Chinese 'wet markets' where they'll eat just about anything. Bat meat is a delicacy and surely bat hunters went into caves looking for their cherished prize, and came out with a world-wide pandemic worthy of a Biblical scale and spread it around.

What were the first images we saw coming out of China? People walking out onto the street and dropping dead on the spot. I contend these deaths could have been from the vaccine trial itself. In fact, it goes to reason that if they were working on COVID in the lab to begin with, they were also working on a vaccine at the same time. After all, the vaccine was 'rolled out' in record time. And in fact, a roll out of its type has never been rolled out in any similar way in the history of medicine.

Could it have been the millions of U.S. tax dollars spent by Anthony Fauci on studying bat coronaviruses in a lab like Wuhan, where it just happened, to first be discovered? Impossible they told us. Repeatedly over and over.

Here's a question, when people didn't seem to like the initial *state sponsored* answer of what happened, what happened next?

Social media kicked in and they shut dissenting opinions down (and to be clear, as I write this even now, this very day, YouTube has once again deleted a video I posted based on 'COVID and vaccine science'.)

Here is AI's take:

The origins of the COVID-19 pandemic have been the subject of intense scrutiny, speculation, and controversy. Initially, many public health officials and media sources suggested that the virus likely emerged from a wet market in Wuhan, China. However, alternative theories, including the possibility of a lab leak from the Wuhan Institute of Virology, gained attention and remain a topic of investigation and debate.

31

Early Assumptions and the Wet Market Theory

In the early days of the COVID-19 pandemic, reports focused on the Huanan Seafood Wholesale Market in Wuhan as the potential source of the outbreak. The market was known to sell live wild animals, leading to speculation that the virus might have jumped from animals to humans in this setting. This narrative was supported by initial investigations and was widely reported in the media.

Shift Towards the Lab Leak Theory

The lab leak theory, which posits that SARS-CoV-2 (the virus causing COVID-19) accidentally escaped from the Wuhan Institute of Virology, gained traction over time. Supporters of this theory pointed to the institute's known research on coronaviruses, the proximity of the lab to the initial outbreak, and changes in the Chinese government's and researchers' behavior regarding inquiries and data sharing.

Former President Donald Trump and some members of his administration publicly suggested the possibility of a lab leak early in the pandemic, which was met with skepticism by many in the scientific community and the media at the time. Critics argued that these claims were not substantiated by clear evidence and were politically motivated.

Dr. Fauci and Funding Controversy

Dr. Anthony Fauci, the director of the National Institute of Allergy and Infectious Diseases (NIAID), became a central figure in the controversy due to his agency's funding of research projects. Some of these projects included grants to the EcoHealth Alliance, a global environmental health research organization, which in turn funded coronavirus research at the Wuhan Institute of Virology.

Critics of Dr. Fauci have raised questions about whether this funding indirectly supported gain-of-function research at the Wuhan lab, which involves manipulating viruses to study their potential impact in humans. Dr. Fauci and others have defended the funding and the research, arguing that it was essential for understanding and preventing pandemics and that safety protocols were followed.

Ongoing Investigations and Lack of Conclusive Evidence

Investigations into the origins of COVID-19, including studies by the World Health Organization (WHO), the U.S. intelligence community, and independent researchers, have not yet provided a definitive answer. Both the wet market and lab leak theories have been considered plausible, but conclusive evidence for either scenario is lacking.

The Chinese government's limited transparency and

reluctance to allow full access to the Wuhan Institute of Virology's records and samples have hindered efforts to clarify the pandemic's origins. This lack of cooperation has fueled further speculation and calls for more thorough, independent investigations.

Impact and Implications

The debate over the origins of COVID-19 has significant implications for public trust in science, international relations, and pandemic preparedness. It has highlighted the challenges of conducting and communicating complex scientific investigations in a highly politicized environment.

The controversy also underscores the importance of open scientific inquiry and collaboration, as well as the need for robust mechanisms to prevent and respond to potential biosafety incidents, whether natural, accidental, or deliberate.

Conclusion

The "COVID wet market" narrative and the competing "lab leak" theory represent the complexities and challenges of determining the origins of a global pandemic. While the wet market theory was initially favored, subsequent developments have led to a reconsideration of the lab leak possibility, with significant public and political ramifications. The truth may remain elusive due to the intertwining of scientific, political, and geopolitical factors. What remains clear is the need for transparent, objective, and collaborative efforts to uncover the origins of COVID-19, not only for historical accuracy but also for future pandemic prevention and preparedness. END

"WEAR YOUR MASK AND LIKE IT!"

Can you imagine that a serious person told you to "wear a mask" to stop an airborne disease "in its tracks"? No study in all of human history has ever shown that it will "stop" anything! Never. But *all of the sudden* these little cloth 'gods' could do what all of humanity could never do – stop air (more on that later) and moving particles of particulate. An insane lie from a bunch of government liars who lie to get rich and lie even more to get even more rich.

Here's AI to discuss:

The narrative surrounding mask usage during the COVID-19 pandemic, particularly in relation to Dr. Anthony Fauci's communications, has been a subject of considerable controversy and debate. This discussion touches on broader issues of public health messaging, trust in government and health officials, and the evolving nature of scientific understanding in the face of a novel virus.

Early Days of the COVID-19 Pandemic

In the initial stages of the COVID-19 outbreak, there was uncertainty and varying guidance about the effectiveness of masks for the general public. Early in 2020, Dr. Fauci, along with other public health officials and organizations, including the World Health Organization (WHO) and the Centers for Disease Control and Prevention (CDC), initially advised against the widespread use of masks by the healthy public, citing the need to reserve supplies for healthcare workers and the lack of evidence at that time supporting their effectiveness in preventing the spread of the virus among the general population.

Changing Guidance on Masks

As the pandemic progressed and more was learned about the virus, especially its asymptomatic transmission, the guidance on mask usage shifted. By April 2020, the CDC and WHO updated their recommendations, advocating for the use of masks in public settings where social distancing measures were difficult to maintain. Dr. Fauci and other health officials began to strongly endorse mask-wearing as a key tool in reducing viral transmission.

The Email Controversy

In the midst of these evolving public health messages, a batch of Dr. Fauci's emails was released under the Freedom of Information Act (FOIA), which included a message from early 2020 where Dr. Fauci advised a recipient that masks were primarily effective for infected individuals to prevent them from spreading the virus to others, and that wearing a mask was not necessary for the general public. Critics seized on this email as evidence that Dr. Fauci believed masks were ineffective while publicly promoting their use, leading to accusations of mixed messaging and eroding public trust.

Context and Interpretation of Fauci's Email

The controversy surrounding Dr. Fauci's email and public statements on masks reflects the complexities of conveying scientific guidance during a rapidly evolving crisis. Proponents of Dr. Fauci argue that his early emails reflected the best available evidence and prevailing scientific consensus at the time and that his public guidance evolved in response to new scientific data about the virus's transmission, particularly asymptomatic and pre-symptomatic spread.

Critics, however, contend that the discrepancy between private correspondence and public statements contributed to confusion and skepticism about the efficacy of masks and the credibility of public health messaging.

The Role of Scientific Adaptability and Communication

The mask debate highlights the challenges faced by public health officials in communicating complex, changing information during a crisis. Effective communication requires not only conveying current knowledge but also transparency about the uncertainty and evolving nature of scientific understanding.

Public health recommendations, especially in a pandemic, must adapt to new evidence. This adaptability is a strength of the scientific process but can be a source of confusion if changes in guidance are not clearly explained to the public.

Impact on Public Trust

The controversies over mask guidance and Dr. Fauci's role have had a significant impact on public trust in health institutions and officials. Trust is essential for public compliance with health guidelines, and inconsistent messaging can undermine efforts to manage public health crises.

Conclusion

The discourse around mask usage, Dr. Fauci's emails, and the broader public health response to COVID-19 underscores the difficulties of science communication in a rapidly evolving situation. It highlights the need for clear, consistent, and transparent communication from public health officials and the importance of basing public health policy on the best available evidence while also acknowledging the limits and uncertainties of current knowledge. In navigating future public health crises, lessons from the mask debate and the COVID-19 pandemic can inform more effective communication strategies and efforts to build and maintain public trust. END

"PLEXIGLASS WILL SAVE US!"

Did you know that the laws of physics stop when there is a plexiglass partition involved?

That's what you were told in this hoax.

Air circulates. The mere action of walking, even slowly, causes air to circulate. But during COVID, if there were a plexiglass partition between you and a bank teller, the circulating air would simply stop circulating altogether! Amazing! How you say? Physics.

Physics is the scientific study of motion and behavior through space and time, but when it came to COVID, the three laws of physics ceased to exist. See, *air knew* that it couldn't traverse over or under any plexiglass structure.

Say you walk into the bank and behind the counter is a teller, but in front of the teller is their plexiglass partition. Air can go above the partition. And there is a hole at the bottom to hand and receive money from the teller - which air can go through as well. So air can travel over and under and *even around the partitions sides* – but no, no it can't! It couldn't! Air knew to stop circulating.

How it knew, no one knows, but the 'science' told us this was real. Trust the science.

AI knows ... something:

During the COVID-19 pandemic, plexiglass barriers became a ubiquitous sight in various settings, from banks and convenience stores to restaurants and offices, as a measure to reduce the spread of the virus. These partitions were intended to act as a physical barrier to respiratory droplets, which are a primary means of COVID-19 transmission. The effectiveness and physics of plexiglass barriers in controlling air circulation and reducing viral spread have been subjects of discussion and study.

The Role of Plexiglass Barriers

Plexiglass partitions are designed to block the direct path of respiratory droplets from one person to another. These droplets, expelled when an infected person coughs, sneezes, talks, or breathes, can carry the SARS-CoV-2 virus. The barriers are not meant to stop air circulation entirely but to

redirect airflow and minimize the risk of droplet
transmission.

Understanding Airflow and Transmission

Airflow and the movement of respiratory droplets in indoor
environments are influenced by various factors, including
air currents, ventilation, the size and behavior of droplets,
and the presence of physical barriers. While plexiglass
barriers can block larger droplets, smaller aerosol particles
can remain suspended in the air and potentially circulate
around or over the barriers.

Physical Principles and Barrier Effectiveness

The effectiveness of plexiglass partitions in preventing
COVID-19 transmission is not about defying the principles of
physics but rather about applying them in ways that reduce
direct exposure to respiratory droplets. The basic physical
principles at play include:

- Aerodynamics of Droplets: Larger droplets tend to fall to the
  ground more quickly due to gravity, while smaller aerosol
  particles can travel longer distances in the air.
- Airflow Patterns: The movement of air in any environment can
  be complex, influenced by ventilation systems, the movement of
  people, and the placement of physical objects, including
  barriers.
- Transmission Dynamics: The risk of COVID-19 transmission
  depends not only on exposure to the virus but also on factors
  like viral load, duration of exposure, and individual

susceptibility.

Studies and Guidelines

Research on the effectiveness of plexiglass barriers has
yielded mixed results. Some studies suggest that when used
correctly, in conjunction with masks and good ventilation,
barriers can help reduce the transmission of larger droplets.
However, other research indicates that in certain
conditions, barriers might disrupt normal airflow patterns
and potentially lead to the accumulation of aerosolized
particles in localized areas.

Guidelines from health organizations have evolved as
understanding of the virus has improved. Initially, when the
focus was primarily on droplet transmission, plexiglass
barriers were widely recommended. As the role of aerosols
in COVID-19 spread became clearer, emphasis shifted
towards the importance of ventilation and air filtration
alongside physical barriers.

Practical Considerations

The installation of plexiglass barriers must consider factors
like size, placement, and the overall configuration of the
space to be effective. Barriers are most effective when they
are positioned to block direct pathways of droplet
transmission between individuals, such as between a
cashier and customer at a store.

However, to address the risk of aerosol transmission, additional measures such as enhanced ventilation, air filtration, and maintaining physical distance are necessary. In some cases, improperly placed barriers can obstruct airflow and potentially create areas where aerosolized virus particles accumulate.

Public Perception and Compliance

Public responses to plexiglass barriers have varied, with some viewing them as a necessary safety measure and others questioning their effectiveness. Compliance with barrier use, as with other COVID-19 mitigation measures, has been influenced by public messaging, trust in scientific guidance, and individual risk assessment.

Conclusion

Plexiglass barriers represent one of many strategies employed to mitigate the spread of COVID-19, based on the principle of blocking direct transmission routes for respiratory droplets. While not a panacea, they can play a role in a multi-faceted approach to reducing transmission risk, especially when combined with other measures like mask-wearing and adequate ventilation. Understanding the physical dynamics of airflow and droplet transmission is crucial in designing and implementing these barriers effectively. As the scientific community's understanding of

COVID-19 transmission has evolved, so too have the recommendations for using barriers in conjunction with other preventive measures to mitigate spread. END

All of this to say nothing more than the idea plexiglass could stop the transmission of any airborne virus maybe, could be, possibly, but probably not, help.

"JUST TAKE THE BLEACH!"

This hoax, still believed by many, is simply another 'smear job' by reporters and the press. If you have seen the clip (and full context) you know the way it was portrayed in the media was nothing but a bold-faced lie. But, liars are gonna lie.

Here's AI discussing:

The claim that President Donald Trump suggested people should inject or ingest bleach or disinfectants to treat COVID-19 represents one of the most widely discussed and controversial moments in the public communication about the pandemic. This claim arose from a press briefing in April 2020, leading to significant public and media discourse about the accuracy and interpretation of Trump's comments.

The Press Briefing Incident

The incident in question occurred during a White House press briefing on April 23, 2020, where President Trump speculated about possible treatments for COVID-19. In the briefing, Trump discussed recent findings presented by

William Bryan, acting head of the U.S. Department of Homeland Security's Science and Technology Directorate, which showed that sunlight, heat, and disinfectants could kill the coronavirus on surfaces and in the air.

Trump suggested exploring the possibility of using light and disinfectant internally to treat the virus, asking if there was a way to do something like that "by injection inside or almost a cleaning." These comments were made in a speculative manner, reflecting Trump's known style of thinking aloud and posing questions to the officials present during the briefings.

Media Interpretation and Public Reaction

The media and public reaction to Trump's comments were swift and widespread. Many news outlets and commentators interpreted his remarks as suggesting that people should inject or ingest disinfectants as a treatment for COVID-19. This interpretation led to widespread criticism and ridicule, with health experts, political figures, and the manufacturers of disinfectant products quickly issuing statements to warn against the ingestion or injection of such substances.

Clarifications and Backlash

In the aftermath of the briefing, President Trump and the White House clarified that he was speaking rhetorically and not suggesting that people should use disinfectants or bleach inside their bodies to treat COVID-19. Despite these clarifications, the narrative that Trump had advised such actions persisted, contributing to the highly charged political and social environment surrounding the pandemic response.

Analysis of the Rhetoric

The controversy highlights the importance of clear communication, especially during a public health crisis. Critics argued that Trump's speculative style and imprecise language led to confusion and potential danger, while supporters contended that his comments were taken out of context and used to unfairly malign him.

The incident underscored the challenges of conveying complex scientific information in press briefings and the potential consequences of misinterpretation or miscommunication. It also demonstrated how statements made by public figures can be quickly amplified and distorted in the public sphere, particularly in a polarized political climate.

Broader Impact on Public Trust and Communication

The "bleach" narrative had broader implications for public trust and the communication between political leaders, the media, and the public. It served as a case study in how easily information can be misconstrued and how quickly misinformation can spread, emphasizing the need for careful and precise language in public health communications.

The incident also fueled debates about the role of the media in interpreting and disseminating information from public officials, with concerns about bias and the potential for media to influence public perception and behavior, especially in the context of a global health emergency.

Conclusion

The claim that President Trump told people to drink bleach to treat COVID-19 was a significant moment in the discourse surrounding the pandemic response. While Trump's comments were speculative and not a direct suggestion to ingest disinfectants, the ensuing media frenzy and public outcry illustrate the critical importance of clear and responsible communication. This episode serves as a reminder of the power of words, the rapid spread of misinformation, and the need for vigilance in media consumption and public discourse. END

COVID KNEW HOW TO TELL TIME!!

If COVID didn't already have enough hoaxes, try this: Another shut down hoax was deciding when to 'open back up'. Many local governments, including the mayor of Nashville, a man named John Cooper, chose the date! And not only that, he *chose a time*! Impressive.

For a long time in Nashville it was 'illegal' to be in a bar past a certain hour.

COVID knew that it couldn't attack you *before* 10pm, but at 10:01pm, you were fair game. In the same way, COVID knew that it could stick around and attack people in the city until a certain date and time, created by decree, by Mayor Cooper. That Cooper was a scientific genius!

But seriously, COVID knew how to tell time.

Here's what AI has to say about it:

The framing of the COVID-19 pandemic, particularly in the

context of government-mandated lockdowns and restrictions and their timed lifting, often led to public and media discourse filled with irony and skepticism. Discussions and jokes about how "COVID knew how to tell time" or how the virus could seemingly adhere to the arbitrary timelines set by political leaders encapsulate a significant aspect of public sentiment during the pandemic. This sentiment underscores a complex interplay between public health directives, political decision-making, and community compliance and skepticism. This essay explores the nuances behind these perceptions and the challenges faced by governments in communicating and implementing COVID-19 restrictions.

The Nature of Government-Imposed Timelines

When the COVID-19 pandemic began to spread globally, governments around the world were tasked with making rapid decisions in the face of a novel, highly contagious virus. The primary tools available to limit the spread of the virus were non-pharmaceutical interventions (NPIs) like social distancing, mask mandates, travel restrictions, and, most disruptively, lockdowns.

Governments often set specific timelines for these restrictions, such as curfews (e.g., no movement between 10 PM and 5 AM), limited hours for businesses (e.g., restaurants closing by 8 PM), and phased re-openings (e.g., "non-essential" businesses can reopen on a specific future date). These measures were typically designed to limit human interactions to reduce the spread of the virus, based on epidemiological models and available data on virus transmission dynamics.

Public Perception and Skepticism

The specificity and seemingly arbitrary nature of some restrictions led to public questioning and humor about the virus's knowledge of these regulations. Phrases like "Does COVID-19 know it should only infect people after 10 PM?" highlight a common skepticism about the rationale behind certain rules. This skepticism was further fueled by instances where policies appeared inconsistent or were poorly explained by officials, leading to confusion and cynicism about the restrictions' effectiveness and intentions.

Challenges in Policy Communication

One of the significant challenges was effectively communicating the reasons behind specific measures. While public health officials understood that no measure could completely stop the virus, the goal was to reduce peak healthcare demand (flattening the curve) and protect the most vulnerable populations until vaccines and more effective treatments became available. However, boiling down complex epidemiological data into guidelines that the general public could easily follow and support was a considerable challenge.

Role of Simplification and Enforcement

Governments often resorted to simplification in public health directives to ensure broad compliance. For instance, setting a curfew after 10 PM does not imply that the virus is less contagious before this time but aims to reduce overall social activity during times when riskier behaviors (like socializing in bars and restaurants) are more likely to occur. Such measures are also easier to enforce than more nuanced and complicated restrictions, which require significant resources to monitor effectively.

Impact of Arbitrary Timelines

Arbitrary timelines for lifting restrictions often coincided with political and economic pressures. Governments had to balance the scientific advice with economic realities and public fatigue with ongoing restrictions. Announcing specific dates for easing restrictions often served as a compromise between ideal public health scenarios and other societal needs. However, these dates could appear as if the virus's behavior would somehow align with these timelines, which contributed to public skepticism.

Scientific Adaptations and Changes

Throughout the pandemic, recommendations and policies evolved as more became known about the virus. This adaptability—essential in scientific inquiry and public health response—sometimes appeared as inconsistency to the public, further complicating trust and compliance. For instance, changes in mask-wearing guidelines were based on accumulating evidence about transmission but were often perceived as flip-flopping.

Conclusion

The notion that "COVID-19 knew how to tell time" is a manifestation of public incredulity towards government-imposed restrictions that often seemed arbitrary or overly simplistic. This sentiment underscores the critical importance of transparent, consistent communication from government and health officials. Explaining the rationale behind specific public health measures, acknowledging their limitations, and adapting policies based on the latest scientific evidence are crucial for maintaining public trust and compliance. As the world continues to navigate the pandemic and future global health challenges, lessons from the communication and implementation missteps during COVID-19 remain relevant. Effective public health management requires not only sound science but also careful consideration of how policies are perceived.

JOE ROGAN - IVERMECTIN

Joe Rogan isn't scared. What's a little horse tranquilizer gonna do?

Oh, that's right. The same drug that's been used for decades, and even won an award for being so effective, went against the Government's propaganda arms – the WHO and CDC. It also went against Pfizer, Johnson & Johnson and others who were scoring a fortune (and immunity from lawsuits) making the junk vaccines. Why take something that could make you well again when you can just pump yourself full of untested concoctions which may (do) cause myocarditis, strokes, stillbirths and more (more on this later)?

AI explains:

The Joe Rogan ivermectin controversy highlights the challenges of medical misinformation, media narratives, and public discourse in the context of the COVID-19 pandemic. In late August 2021, Joe Rogan, a prominent podcast host and media personality, announced he had tested positive for COVID-19 and was taking several medications, including ivermectin, to treat his symptoms. This led to widespread media coverage and public debate, often focusing on the use of ivermectin, a drug more commonly associated with veterinary medicine in popular discourse, despite its long-standing approval for certain human uses.

Joe Rogan's COVID-19 Treatment Announcement

Rogan revealed on his podcast, "The Joe Rogan Experience," that he contracted COVID-19 and was following a treatment regimen that included ivermectin, monoclonal antibodies, prednisone, and other medications. He claimed to have improved rapidly after starting this regimen. Rogan's mention of ivermectin, particularly, sparked a flurry of media attention and controversy.

Misrepresentation and Media Reaction

Following Rogan's announcement, many media outlets and commentators quickly focused on his use of ivermectin, with some erroneously reporting that he had taken a "horse dewormer" or "horse tranquilizer." This mischaracterization stemmed from ivermectin's well-known use in veterinary medicine, particularly for deworming horses, despite its also having applications for treating specific human ailments.

Ivermectin, an anti-parasitic medication, was approved for human use by the U.S. Food and Drug Administration (FDA) in the 1980s and has been used to treat conditions like river blindness and intestinal strongyloidiasis. It won the Nobel Prize for Medicine in 2015 for its contributors to treating parasitic diseases. However, during the COVID-19 pandemic, ivermectin gained attention as a potential treatment for the virus, leading to public and medical debate over its efficacy and safety in this context.

Public and Professional Response

The media's portrayal of Rogan's use of ivermectin as a "horse dewormer" led to public confusion and ridicule, overshadowing a more nuanced discussion about the drug's use and research related to COVID-19. Medical professionals and health organizations, including the FDA and the World Health Organization (WHO), advised against using ivermectin to treat COVID-19 outside of clinical trials, citing insufficient evidence for its effectiveness against the virus and potential health risks from improper dosing.

Rogan criticized the media's coverage of his treatment, accusing them of spreading misinformation and sensationalizing his use of ivermectin. He highlighted the drug's legitimate medical uses in humans and expressed concern over the media's role in distorting the narrative.

Impact on Public Discourse and Trust

The controversy over Rogan's use of ivermectin and the subsequent media coverage exemplify the broader challenges of communicating medical information during a public health crisis. The incident became a flash point in discussions about media credibility, scientific literacy, and public trust in health advice. It underscored the difficulties in navigating the complex landscape of medical treatment options for COVID-19, where emerging research, political ideologies, and media narratives often intersect and conflict.

Ethical and Societal Considerations

The Joe Rogan ivermectin story raises important questions about the responsibilities of public figures, the media, and medical professionals in disseminating health-related information. The rapid spread of misleading information about ivermectin's use and safety highlights the need for accurate, balanced, and context-aware reporting, especially during a global health emergency.

Conclusion

The narrative surrounding Joe Rogan's announcement of using ivermectin for COVID-19 treatment illustrates the tension between medical science, media representation, and public perception. While ivermectin is a medication with legitimate uses in humans, its promotion as a treatment for COVID-19 without strong supporting evidence has led to controversy and confusion. The episode with Rogan brought to light the challenges of communicating nuanced medical information to the public and the role of the media in shaping those discussions, emphasizing the need for careful, evidence-based reporting in health journalism. END

"PEAK OIL!?! OH NO!"

Of all the dumb things to ever come out of the media and Democrats is this idea of "peak oil". Talk about a hoax!

The truth is, the world is drenched in oil! It's everywhere. It isn't a 'fossil fuel', it's a naturally occurring, ever present part of Earth. And everything we have comes from the Earth (as I will continue to say).

There is literally a 0% chance the world ever runs out of oil. If we can get it, we can have it. But the media and Democrats don't want you to have it because, *"oil bad!"*.

So what was "peak oil" if you don't know? AI explains:

The discourse around climate change and related phenomena like peak oil has been marked by evolving narratives, predictions, and debates over the decades. While it is inaccurate to label climate change itself as a hoax— given the broad scientific consensus on its reality and human-driven causes (keep this in mind for later)—the discussion around specific aspects like peak oil has seen a

range of predictions, some of which have not come to pass
as expected.

Understanding Peak Oil

Peak oil refers to the point in time when the extraction of oil
reaches its maximum rate, after which production will
irreversibly decline. The concept gained prominence in the
scientific and economic communities as a way to highlight
the finite nature of fossil fuel resources and the need for
alternative energy sources.

Historical Predictions and Outcomes

Predictions about when peak oil would occur have varied,
influenced by factors like technological advancements,
economic changes, and new discoveries of oil reserves:

- In the 1960s and 1970s, concerns about depleting oil reserves
  and the ability to meet growing energy demands led to
  predictions that peak oil would occur in the near future. For
  example, in 1966, some believed that peak oil would be reached
  by 1976.
- During the 1970s, following the oil crises, further predictions
  suggested peak oil would occur in the early 1990s.
- In the 1980s, amidst economic fluctuations and changing energy
  markets, predictions often pointed to the early 2000s as the
  likely period for peak oil.
- By the 1990s and into the 2000s, some analyses extended the
  timeline further, suggesting peak oil might occur in the 2020s or
  beyond.

Shifts in the Energy Landscape

The concept of peak oil has had to contend with significant shifts in the global energy landscape, including:

- Technological Advances: Improvements in extraction technologies, like hydraulic fracturing and deep-sea drilling, have made previously inaccessible reserves available, delaying the onset of peak oil.
- Alternative Energy Sources: The rise of renewable energy sources, such as wind, solar, and biofuels, has begun to reduce dependence on oil, changing consumption patterns and impacting peak oil timelines.
- Economic and Political Factors: Fluctuations in global markets, political instability in key oil-producing regions, and policy decisions related to climate change and energy production have all influenced oil production and consumption trends.

Climate Change and the Energy Debate

The discussion of peak oil is closely tied to broader concerns about climate change and the transition to a sustainable energy future. While the timing of peak oil remains uncertain and subject to various influencing factors, the imperative to reduce reliance on fossil fuels to mitigate climate change is a central theme in scientific and policy discussions.

- From Peak Oil to Climate Action: The focus has shifted from concerns about running out of oil to worries about the consequences of burning it, emphasizing the need to reduce greenhouse gas emissions and transition to cleaner energy sources.

Critiques and Controversies

The narrative around peak oil and its evolving timelines has faced criticism and skepticism, with some viewing the changing predictions as evidence of alarmism or flawed analyses. However, these shifts often reflect the complex, dynamic nature of global energy systems and the difficulty of making long-term predictions in the face of technological, economic, and political changes.

Conclusion

The discourse on peak oil and its relation to climate change exemplifies the challenges of predicting and managing global environmental and energy trends. While earlier predictions of peak oil have frequently been pushed back, the broader issue remains the need for a sustainable transition away from fossil fuels to address climate change. The ongoing debate and evolving narratives around peak oil reflect the complexities of these intertwined global challenges. END

"THE CONSENSUS"

When I think about climate change the first thing I actually think about is how wrong the predictions have been throughout the years.

In the late 1960's into the early 1970's the fear was global cooling would happen. And the fear mongering began. To be clear, this fear mongering (hoax setup) was actually an admission that more people die from the cold than from extreme heat, but you wouldn't guess that today.

Today we have a prepubescent teen talking to adults like they are the children and excoriating them with 'how dare you!".

In 2010 Bill Gates stood on a TED stage and gave a speech, "One Wish". In this speech, which became viral for a number of reasons, there was one thing that stuck out to me personally. He said, "If you gave me only one wish for the next 50 years; I could pick who's president, I could pick a vaccine which is something I love, or, I could pick that this thing that's half the costs with no CO_2 gets invited, this is the wish I would pick." So I went to work.

I wanted to invent this thing. Not because I believed in all the climate change gobble-de-gook, but because I thought, "why not?".

Fast forward 10 years and I'm in negotiations with a major 'climate' university about making a pitch to them for the use of their research facility, a small team of people, and resources to help make 'my one wish' a reality.

After a long and protracted negotiation about making the pitch we finally signed the legal documents I needed in order to ensure I could make the pitch without my invention being stolen outright by the university. I signed the papers; they and their legal team signed the papers; and finally I was able to go in and make the pitch.

It was decided that the two Chairs of the environmental department would be the professors I would meet with. It would be in a private meeting room, no electronics would be allowed (listening devices, recording equipment) and even cell phones weren't allowed.

Here's what I didn't know - one of the professors was a

'solar' guy. The other, a 'geothermal' guy.

So we all meet and get off to a cordial start. Eventually after hooking up my computer to their equipment, the lights came down and my presentation began.

Within about 15 minutes, "geo-guy" fell asleep in his chair.

Within about 16 minutes, "solar guy" started arguing with me about some of the things I said about solar.

In the presentation I spoke about all the current forms of electricity generation, and broke down what was wrong with each. For instance, both solar and wind need 'farms' - meaning in order to power a bunch of homes and businesses, you need a lot of land.

What happens to solar panels when a hail storm comes? You may guess, they get shattered. This happened not too long ago to a solar farm - shattering hundreds of panels, costing millions of dollars, and of course, the loss of electricity.

With geo-guy still sound asleep in his chair, I finally moved into the second part of the screen presentation and described, in full, how my system would work, what it would do, and why it met Bill Gates' One Wish of ½ the costs and no Co2.

Solar guy seemed none-to-impressed. The lights came on, geo-guy woke up for a moment, and I moved my presentation to the chalkboard where I began writing out all the mathematics, in very simple terms, of the system.

The system uses existing technology. The technology has been proven to work - just with my system, it would work differently. And better. It would 'deliver'.

The system didn't break the laws of physics. The science remained intact.

The laws of math weren't stretched to become unrecognizable, and in fact, the math worked as simple as saying 2+2=4.

And last, the engineering, what really set the system apart from all other systems, was flawless - and what really helped my system do what it was meant to do.

S.T.E.M. complete.

What do you think happened?

Geo-guy started arguing that geo was better. Solar guy started arguing the math was flawed and solar could make up for its low pass-thru rate. Neither even tried to grasp what I had just outlined, they only cared about what they cared about - and that was the end of that.

It was 2 hours overall, and it was a complete and total waste of time. *These people aren't serious.* There's a grift going on and to solve any one problem would end their portion of the grift (this university gets millions in grants and donations, and at the time of our meeting had even just finished placing a new multi-million dollar wing on the school to 'study' the environment and 'solve' the energy problem).

I'll give you another example: There is a very popular TED-like conference here in Florida where some of the biggest, brightest, and most well known people come to bloviate over finding a *solution* to some of the problems we face.

I wrote to the founder of the conference and asked, 'What if you didn't have to imagine a solution to something and someone simply solved the problem?' - with my thought being I could go and discuss how this one particular problem was 'solved'. He wrote back and essentially said, "that's not what we do".

It's not about solving problems or finding a solution - it's about the grift. Solve too many problems, or even one, and suddenly people start to lose money and influence.

The climate crowd are not very serious people. And in fact, I'm not sure how, or why, they've been listened to for more than 40 years.

The truth is, global warming and climate change isn't that big a deal. CO_2 is a good thing. Warmer temps have saved a lot of lives. But even if it were a problem, they still wouldn't care to solve the issue. Trust me, I solved a small part of the problem and literally no one would listen. But why listen when your pockets are lined with grant money to just keep on 'studying' the 'problem'?

Once AI emerged I used it to run the numbers, and guess

what? Exactly what you'd expect - everything came out *perfectly*. What took me 10 or so years to create, it proved in around 20 minutes – and even said it (un-prompted) how I say it!

I said earlier the everything comes from the ground. Everything we have. Everything that humans make. Everything that makes anything that humans make - everything.

That literally anything would be 'bad for the environment' is something so completely idiotic it's hard to even put words to. We don't even understand "the environment" to begin with!

I'll provide an example using Mars (of all places):

Recently, the Mars module completed an experiment on the surface of Mars where it was able to create oxygen to disperse on the planet. With humans wanting to go to Mars, and Mars being 90+% made of carbon, it makes sense humans would need the oxygen should anyone on Earth ever make it there. But have they considered:

According to these people, the reason Earth is 'dying' is because humans live on Earth, and all the terrible things we pump into the atmosphere is, therefore, killing the planet. So then how smart is it for humans to begin killing Mars' atmosphere before humans even arrive?

Secondly, we've all heard of "Martians". Growing up we were treated almost daily to stories about Martians and how we know, but don't know, but could, but might be, on Mars.

What if Martians were real and did breathe carbon the same as we breathe oxygen - and need it to survive? Do these people want to go to Mars to colonize and wipe out another race of extra-planetary citizens? Seems so.

But you see, it's okay for them to create havoc on *another* planet and potential species for their ultimate goal of making Mars a viable place for humans to live - they just don't want to allow us to make a viable place for humans to live because oil, the main drivers of our entire ability to have good lives, "damages" the only viable place humans have to live.

If this doesn't make sense, it's not supposed to. You're

supposed to just bow down to their preeminence and how smart they are to be the overlords of you and your family.

In 3-400 years, when humans may make it to Mars, I sure hope at least a few "Mars environmental supporters" make the trip too and be as big a pain in the butt as these same people have been to the rest of us here on Earth. Maybe they'll all run out of oxygen, they won't totally kill the planet, and it's current inhabitants can live peacefully and safe from humans, forever.

Here's what AI says about "consensus":

The debate around climate change, particularly the notion of a scientific consensus and the assertion that "the science is settled," touches on broader themes of scientific understanding, consensus-building, and public communication. Critics of the mainstream climate change narrative often argue that the discourse around consensus can oversimplify complex scientific processes and stifle ongoing inquiry and debate.

The Notion of Consensus in Science

In scientific terms, a consensus generally refers to a

situation where there is a widespread agreement among experts in a particular field, based on a body of evidence that has been subjected to rigorous testing and validation. In the context of climate change, the consensus often cited is that the Earth is warming and that human activities, particularly the emission of greenhouse gases like carbon dioxide, are a significant contributing factor.

One frequently referenced study in discussions of consensus is the 2013 paper by John Cook and colleagues, which analyzed the abstracts of nearly 12,000 peer-reviewed climate science papers and found that 97% of those that expressed a position on the cause of global warming endorsed the view that humans are responsible.

Critiques of the Consensus Argument

Critics of the climate change consensus argue that the methodology of studies like Cook's can be flawed or misleading. They point out issues such as the classification of papers, the definition of consensus, and the potential for bias in selecting and interpreting studies. Additionally, they highlight that not all scientists or studies unequivocally support the consensus view, suggesting that there is more diversity of opinion than is often portrayed.

The argument against the notion of settled science in climate change also draws on the philosophy of science, which emphasizes skepticism, continuous questioning, and the provisional nature of scientific knowledge. Critics assert that science is inherently dynamic and that claiming a topic is settled can hinder progress and the exploration of alternative hypotheses and explanations.

Historical Perspectives on Scientific Consensus

The history of science is replete with examples where established consensuses were challenged and revised in light of new evidence. The flat Earth theory, the geocentric model of the solar system, and the phlogiston theory of combustion are all historical examples where scientific consensus shifted dramatically as new discoveries emerged.

Critics of the current climate change consensus often draw parallels with these historical examples, arguing that just as past consensuses were overturned, so too could the current understanding of climate change. They caution against the hubris of assuming that current scientific understandings are infallible.

The Role of Continuous Discovery in Science

Science advances through a process of hypothesis generation, testing, and revision. This ongoing cycle of discovery means that scientific knowledge is always evolving, and what is considered a consensus at one time may change as new data and insights emerge.

In the realm of climate science, this means that while there is a strong consensus on many aspects of climate change, there are still areas of uncertainty and active research, such as the full range of climate sensitivity to greenhouse gases, the impact of clouds and aerosols, and the interactions of various components of the Earth system.

The Impact of Public Communication and Policy

The way in which the climate change debate is communicated to the public and policymakers can have significant implications. While the idea of a scientific consensus can be a powerful tool for advocating for policy action, it can also be a double-eded sword if it leads to the perception that all debate is closed, potentially undermining public trust in science if the narrative is seen as dismissing alternative views or new findings.

Effective communication about climate change and scientific consensus should convey the robust evidence supporting the consensus view while also acknowledging areas of ongoing research and uncertainty. This approach can help maintain the credibility of the scientific community and foster a more nuanced public understanding of the issue.

Conclusion

The discourse around the climate change consensus and the notion of settled science reflects the complexities of scientific knowledge and public communication. While there is a strong consensus among climate scientists about the basics of climate change, particularly regarding the role of human activities in driving recent warming, science is an ever-evolving process of discovery and understanding. Acknowledging the nuances, uncertainties, and dynamic nature of scientific inquiry is crucial in fostering a balanced and informed public discourse on climate change and other scientific issues. END

THE POPULATION KILLER (WOULDN'T START WITH HIMSELF)

Once again we're hearing people, who themselves refuse to die, talking about how many people are on Earth and how, just like in the 1970's, we will be "unable" to feed them all. As John Stossel says, "give me a break". The only thing that's going to stop people from eating are the globalists and their "de-farm" agenda.

Oh, you've not heard of this? Well, once again it comes down to "climate" as they see it. Because of the climate and that nasty global warming, we have to end farming. Cows, pigs, hogs, and chickens should be replaced by bugs.

Yes, bugs. We should all eat bugs and be happy.

How does this even make any sense? Well, to the left's mentally deranged "climate warrior", farming contributes XX amount of carbon into the atmosphere and because of this, it's defeating their plans to get to 'net 0'; that venerated belief in *their religion* that that's what we need to get to in order to 'save the planet'.

The "Population Bomb" is a book written by Paul Ehrlich and published in 1968, which predicted disastrous levels of overpopulation leading to mass starvation and societal collapse within the next few decades if unchecked. The book begins with a dramatic statement: "The battle to feed all of humanity is over." This line set the tone for the dire predictions that followed, which were based on the Malthusian theory that population growth would outstrip food production. Ehrlich's alarmist tone and stark warnings had a significant influence on public discourse about population and the environment during the 1970s and beyond, but many of his predictions did not materialize, leading to debates about the validity and impact of his projections.

Background and Thesis of "The Population Bomb"

Paul Ehrlich, a biologist by training, argued in "The Population Bomb" that human overpopulation was the greatest threat facing humanity and that if the population continued to increase at the current rates, it would result in severe shortages of food, space, and resources. Ehrlich's predictions included famine and death on a massive scale, with the 1970s and 1980s being particularly critical decades as he predicted they would see major food scarcities and social upheavals as a result.

Predictions and Proposals

Ehrlich's book contained several extreme predictions and dire scenarios that painted a bleak future:

- He suggested that hundreds of millions of people would starve to death in the 1970s.
- He believed that countries like India were essentially doomed to suffer massive famines.
- Ehrlich also proposed radical measures to avert catastrophe, including population control policies that ranged from voluntary family planning to more coercive measures, such as "compulsory birth regulation."

Criticism and Scientific Scrutiny

The dire predictions of "The Population Bomb" did not come to pass. Ehrlich's forecasted famines and massive death tolls due to overpopulation were not realized to the extent he predicted. Several factors contributed to this:

- Advances in agricultural technology, known as the Green Revolution, significantly increased food production through the use of new crop varieties and agricultural techniques, countering the food shortages Ehrlich predicted.
- Improvements in healthcare and disease prevention also helped to manage population growth rates in many regions of the world more effectively than anticipated.
- Economic development in many countries led to lower birth

rates, aligning with the demographic transition theory which posits that as countries develop economically, their rates of population growth tend to decrease.

Critics have also pointed out that Ehrlich's approach was overly simplistic and failed to account for human innovation and complex socio-economic factors that influence population growth and food production. Furthermore, his support for coercive population control measures has been widely criticized for ethical reasons.

Impact and Legacy

Despite its flawed predictions, "The Population Bomb" had a lasting impact on public policy and environmental discourse. It helped to catalyze the modern environmental movement, influencing discussions and policies related to resource conservation, environmental protection, and family planning. The book was instrumental in raising awareness about the potential environmental consequences of unchecked population growth, even if the solutions it proposed and the predictions it made were controversial or incorrect.

Ehrlich's work also contributed to the establishment of organizations and conferences dedicated to addressing global population growth as a part of environmental and resource management strategies. It spurred research into sustainable agricultural practices and helped shift public policies towards greater support for family planning services worldwide.

Re-evaluation and Current Views

In recent years, scholars and environmentalists have re-evaluated the predictions and policy recommendations made in "The Population Bomb." While Ehrlich's overarching thesis about the dangers of overpopulation is taken seriously by some, others argue that the focus should be on consumption patterns, particularly in developed countries, and on sustainable development practices rather than on controlling population growth alone.

Conclusion

"The Population Bomb" by Paul Ehrlich, while criticized for its inaccuracies and alarmist tone, played a significant role in shaping the discourse around population growth and environmental sustainability. It is a pivotal work in the environmental movement, serving both as a cautionary tale about the prediction of doomsday scenarios and as a catalyst for bringing population issues into conversations about global sustainability. As the world continues to face complex environmental challenges, the lessons from the reception and impact of "The Population Bomb" remain relevant in discussions about how best to balance human needs with the planet's ability to sustain life. END

KIDS IN CAGES

Um ... it was OBAMA.

Let's let AI explain:

The issue of "kids in cages" at the U.S. southern border has been a contentious and emotional topic in American politics, particularly highlighted during the Trump administration. The term became a flash point in the broader debate over immigration policies, human rights, and the treatment of migrants, especially unaccompanied minors.

Historical Context

The practice of detaining undocumented immigrants, including children, in secure facilities has been a part of U.S. immigration enforcement for many years, spanning multiple administrations. During the Obama administration, there was a significant increase in the number of unaccompanied minors and family units arriving at the U.S. border, leading to challenges in processing and detaining these individuals. In response, the Department of Homeland Security (DHS) expanded the use of detention facilities.

Photos from this period, showing children sleeping in

fenced enclosures, were later used to criticize the Trump administration, though some of these images were mistakenly attributed to Trump's policies when they were actually taken during Obama's presidency.

Trump Administration Policies

The issue of "kids in cages" gained heightened attention during President Donald Trump's tenure, particularly in relation to the "Zero Tolerance" policy announced in April 2018. This policy mandated the criminal prosecution of all adults illegally entering the country, leading to the separation of children from their parents or adult family members, as the adults were detained and the children placed in the custody of the Department of Health and Human Services (HHS).

The images and reports of children being held in cage-like structures in detention facilities, coupled with the policy of family separation, sparked widespread public outrage. Critics argued that these practices were inhumane and traumatizing for the children. The term "kids in cages" became a symbol of what many saw as the cruel immigration policies of the Trump administration.

Media Coverage and Public Reaction

Media coverage of the issue was intense, with many reports focusing on the conditions in the detention facilities and the emotional impact of the separation on children. The narrative often framed the Trump administration as the initiator of the practice of detaining children in cage-like conditions, although similar facilities had been used in previous administrations.

The public reaction included widespread protests, legal challenges, and calls for policy change. Prominent political figures, activists, and celebrities visited the border facilities, drawing further attention to the issue.

Alexandria Ocasio-Cortez's Involvement

Congresswoman Alexandria Ocasio-Cortez (AOC) became one of the most vocal critics of the detention practices. Her visit to a border facility and subsequent emotional testimony, claiming she saw migrants drinking water out of toilets (a claim that was contested), added to the controversy and media attention. Her use of the term "concentration camps" to describe the detention facilities further ignited public debate and criticism.

Policy Reversals and Continued Challenges

The backlash against the family separation policy led President Trump to sign an executive order in June 2018 ending the practice. However, the issue of how to manage and house unaccompanied minors and families at the border remained a significant challenge.

Detention practices continued to be a point of contention, with ongoing debates about the conditions in the facilities, the legality of detaining minors, and the best approaches to handling asylum seekers and undocumented migrants, especially families with children.

Legacy and Ongoing Issues

The "kids in cages" narrative contributed to a broader discussion about immigration policy, human rights, and the treatment of minors in the immigration enforcement process. It highlighted the complexities of border management, the humanitarian concerns involved, and the political difficulties in finding lasting solutions to these issues.

Under the Biden administration, efforts were made to move away from detention in favor of alternative methods of monitoring migrants, such as ankle bracelets or case management programs. However, the influx of unaccompanied minors and families at the border continued to pose significant logistical and humanitarian challenges.

Conclusion

The "kids in cages" controversy illustrates the highly charged nature of U.S. immigration policy and the difficulties in balancing border security with humanitarian concerns. While the Trump administration faced significant criticism for its handling of migrant children, the use of detention facilities and the broader challenges of immigration enforcement have been issues for successive U.S. administrations. The ongoing debate underscores the need for comprehensive immigration reform and more humane and effective policies for managing migration and supporting asylum seekers and undocumented immigrants, particularly vulnerable children. END

TEXAS BORDER PATROL WHIPPING ILLEGAL MIGRANTS ENTERING AMERICA

In September 2021, images and narratives emerged from the U.S.-Mexico border near Del Rio, Texas, that sparked widespread controversy and heated political debate. The incident involved U.S. Border Patrol agents on horseback confronting Haitian migrants trying to enter the United States. Some media outlets and public figures interpreted the agents' actions as using whips against the migrants. This interpretation led to significant public outrage, accusations of racism and inhumanity, and calls for accountability. However, the narrative that agents used whips was later contested and clarified, revealing complexities in media reporting and the politicization of border security issues.

Initial Incident and Media Coverage

The controversy began when photographs and video footage circulated showing Border Patrol agents on horseback attempting to deter Haitian migrants from crossing into the United States. The imagery showed agents swinging long reins while maneuvering their horses to block and turn back migrants near the riverbank.

These images were quickly picked up by major news outlets and social media, with some commentators and public figures describing the agents' actions as using "whips" against the migrants. This narrative suggested that the agents were deliberately whipping the migrants, evoking historical images of slavery and violent oppression.

Public and Political Reaction

The interpretation of the events led to an immediate outcry. Prominent Democrats, including members of Congress and Vice President Kamala Harris, expressed horror and condemned the actions seen in the photos and videos. President Joe Biden also commented on the incident, promising that the agents involved would face consequences, stating, "It's wrong, it's ugly, and it's not American."

The narrative of Border Patrol agents using whips was used to critique not only the specific actions of the agents involved but also broader U.S. immigration policies and practices, which critics argued were inhumane and racially biased.

Clarifications and Challenges to the Initial Narrative

As more information became available, the narrative that

Border Patrol agents had used whips on migrants began to be questioned. Officials from the Department of Homeland Security (DHS) and the Border Patrol clarified that the agents were holding horse reins, not whips, and that the reins were used to control the horses, not to strike migrants.

Photographers and journalists who were at the scene also clarified that they did not witness agents whipping anyone. The photographer who took the viral images explained that while the photos might have appeared to show agents whipping people, he saw no migrants being struck by the reins.

Investigation and Policy Responses

The Biden administration faced pressure to respond to the incident swiftly. DHS Secretary Alejandro Mayorkas announced an investigation into the agents' conduct to determine the appropriate disciplinary actions. The use of horses in border patrol operations in Del Rio was temporarily suspended.

This incident underscored the challenges and criticisms faced by the Biden administration regarding its handling of border security and immigration, particularly concerning the treatment of Haitian migrants, thousands of whom were encamped under a bridge in Del Rio around the same time.

Media Reflections and Ethical Considerations

The incident raised significant questions about the role of media in shaping public perceptions of complex events. The rapid spread of the initial, incorrect narrative highlighted the potential consequences of reporting in real-time, especially in politically and emotionally charged situations. Media outlets and journalists faced scrutiny over their responsibility to verify information before dissemination and the impact of their reporting on public opinion and policy.

The event also sparked discussions about the ethical implications of immigration enforcement and the treatment of migrants at the border. It brought to light the often harsh realities of border control measures and the human stories behind migration.

Conclusion

The narrative of Texas Border Patrol agents whipping Haitian migrants, though later debunked, had a lasting impact on public discourse surrounding immigration and border enforcement in the United States. It highlighted the complexities of border management, the challenges in media reporting, and the deep political and ideological divides over how to handle immigration. Ultimately, the incident served as a critical moment for reflecting on the narratives that shape public policy and opinion,

underscoring the need for careful, nuanced journalism and
informed public discussion about border security and
human rights. END

JUSSIE SMOLLETT

What was the first thing that led you to believe that the Jussie Smollett incident wasn't real?

Was it the fact that it happened at 2:00 or 3:00 in the morning?

That would be a sure giveaway if you're anybody with a certain type of brain which says that Trump supporters have jobs. They actually go to work, and do work, and make the economy work throughout the day. Which means that they have no time to be out on the streets in Chicago at 2:00 a.m. in the morning.

If you believed the Jussie Smollett incident was real, it's probably because you have more time on your hands than any single average Trump supporter. And aside from that, Trump supporters don't really get in the face of those that they disagree with, or dislike. The fact is the left in America and all around the world are the only people - in the entire world - that take such measures. So I knew from the beginning that this Jussie situation was not adding up. And though the media would have you believe that Trump supporters, MAGA lovers, MAGA hat wearing people would go so far as to *attack* someone at 2:00 in the morning, on a Street in Chicago, also told me it was a lie.

This is what AI has to say about it:

The Jussie Smollett case became one of the most controversial and talked-about incidents in recent years, intertwining issues of race, politics, and media representation. Smollett, an actor on the TV show "Empire," reported to Chicago police in January 2019 that he was the victim of a hate crime. The case took numerous twists and turns, ultimately leading to Smollett's conviction for filing a false police report.

The Alleged Attack

On January 29, 2019, Jussie Smollett reported that he was attacked by two men in downtown Chicago. According to Smollett, the attackers made racial and homophobic slurs, referenced "MAGA Country" (a reference to Donald Trump's "Make America Great Again" slogan), put a noose around his neck, and poured a chemical substance on him. The allegations immediately sparked widespread media attention and public outrage, with celebrities and politicians expressing support for Smollett and condemning the attackers.

Initial Investigation and Public Reaction

The Chicago Police Department began an investigation, treating the incident as a potential hate crime. The media extensively covered the story, with debates about the rise of hate crimes in the United States. Public sympathy was initially with Smollett, who gave an emotional interview on ABC's "Good Morning America," affirming the details of his account and expressing frustration at disbelief over his narrative.

Turning Point in the Case

The case took a significant turn when the Chicago Police Department announced that the investigation's trajectory had shifted based on interviews with two brothers, Abel and Ola Osundairo, who were previously considered suspects. Reports emerged that Smollett might have known the brothers and allegedly paid them to stage the attack. Surveillance footage, financial transactions, and testimonies aligned to suggest that the assault was orchestrated.

Charges and Legal Proceedings

In February 2019, Smollett was charged with filing a false police report, a felony charge. The case sparked debates on the reliability of hate crime reporting, the media's role in shaping narratives, and the political implications of the alleged "MAGA" connection. Smollett pleaded not guilty, maintaining his innocence and insisting that the attack was real and not orchestrated.

The legal proceedings experienced twists, including the initial set of charges being dropped in March 2019, leading to public outcry and confusion. The case was revisited, and in February 2020, Smollett faced new charges related to the incident, reflecting ongoing legal and public scrutiny.

Trial and Conviction

Jussie Smollett's trial took place in late 2021. The prosecution argued that Smollett staged the attack to gain publicity and sympathy, leveraging the political and social climate. The defense maintained that Smollett was a victim of a real hate crime and that the Osundairo brothers' testimonies were motivated by financial gain.

In December 2021, Smollett was found guilty on five counts of disorderly conduct for filing a false police report. The trial revealed extensive details of the planning and execution of the supposed attack, including text messages and financial transactions between Smollett and the Osundairo brothers.

Sentencing and Aftermath

In March 2022, Smollett was sentenced to 150 days in jail, 30 months of felony probation, restitution to the city of Chicago, and a fine. The sentence aimed to address both the false reporting and the broader implications of the case on public trust and resources. Smollett's legal team announced plans to appeal, maintaining his innocence.

Impact and Reflections

The Jussie Smollett case left a lasting impact on public discourse around hate crimes, media responsibility, and the intersections of race, sexuality, and politics. The initial support for Smollett, followed by the backlash after the revelation of the hoax, highlighted the complexities and sensitivities of addressing hate crimes in a polarized societal and political environment.

Critics argued that the case damaged the credibility of legitimate hate crime victims and exploited serious social issues for personal gain. Supporters of Smollett, while fewer after the trial, suggested that the case was emblematic of broader systemic biases and injustices.

Conclusion

The Jussie Smollett case is a multifaceted saga that encapsulates numerous contemporary issues, including the media's role in shaping narratives, the political and social significance of hate crime allegations, and the legal system's handling of high-profile cases. It serves as a cautionary tale about the consequences of fabricating crimes and the complex interplay between personal actions and broader societal dynamics. END

BUBBA WALLACE

Bubba Wallace is a race car driver. He races in the NASCAR Cup Series which is primarily seen on Fox television.

He also just happens to be African-American. One of the few African-American's in NASCAR's upper echelon.

So why would he think - after being in the series for a number of years - that someone would hang a noose on his garage door?

Maybe he's not the one that actually found the "noose", or reported the noose, or got the media, the FBI, and law enforcement involved. Maybe not personally. But how is it even a possibility that the people that do work in his name would believe the NASCAR fans and other race teams are a bunch of low life, worthless, racists? Could it be because of the whole "DEI" push in NASCAR? Where there are now 'victims', and 'victims' need to have a victim mentality? Most likely. After all, no crash is his fault (and he's in more than most drivers it seems). It MUST be ... ya know.

For the fans of NASCAR it was a monumental hoax.

People who love NASCAR - the people that watch NASCAR and go to the races - are sick of DEI ESG BLM and whatever other acronym there is - and they don't want it shoved down their throats. And with this hoax we saw ourselves *all* having some grievance shoved down our throats.

If you followed along in the story you know that the noose was just a hand tie to pull the garage door down and wasn't a noose at all. Everyone involved in cars - everyone around a garage - at some time in their life has seen a hand tied pull-down for a garage door. Not Bubba! Or at least, none of his team ever had, it seemed. Amazing. No, they had to get an investigation going. They had to figure out who the racists were! And if it was a *hate crime* (of all things!).

Give us a break.

Here's what AI has to say:

The Bubba Wallace incident in June 2020 became a significant event in NASCAR's history, intertwining the worlds of sports, race relations, and media perception.

Wallace, the only full-time African American driver in NASCAR's elite Cup Series at the time, was thrust into the national spotlight after a rope fashioned like a noose was found in his garage stall at Talladega Superspeedway in Alabama.

Background and Incident

Bubba Wallace had been an advocate for racial equality and had successfully campaigned for NASCAR to ban the Confederate flag at its events, a move that marked a significant shift in the sport's approach to issues of race and identity. The discovery of the noose was initially perceived as a racially motivated threat against Wallace, especially in the context of the heightened awareness and activism following the murder of George Floyd.

Immediate Reaction

The report of the noose led to an outpouring of support for Wallace from fellow drivers, teams, and fans, culminating in a poignant moment before a race at Talladega where drivers and team members pushed Wallace's car to the front of the grid in a show of solidarity. The incident attracted widespread media coverage, with public figures and politicians weighing in on the implications for NASCAR and the broader societal struggle against racism.

FBI Investigation and Findings

The FBI was quickly involved to determine whether a hate crime had been committed. After a thorough investigation, the FBI concluded that the rope fashioned like a noose had been present in that particular garage stall since at least October 2019, long before the garage was assigned to Wallace for the race weekend. The investigation found that Wallace was not the target of a hate crime, as the noose-like rope was determined to be a garage door pull rope that had been there for months.

Public and Media Response

The FBI's conclusion sparked a complex public and media reaction. Some people viewed the incident as a misunderstanding or overreaction, while others saw it as indicative of the racial tensions and fears that permeate American society. Critics argued that the incident was hastily labeled a hate crime without sufficient evidence, leading to debates about the prevalence and perception of racism in the United States.

Wallace faced a backlash from some quarters, with accusations that the incident was a hoax or staged, despite the FBI's finding that he had not been involved in the creation or reporting of the noose. He defended his and NASCAR's response to the incident, emphasizing the importance of taking potential threats seriously, especially in the context of America's racial climate.

NASCAR's Response

NASCAR, having conducted its own investigation alongside the FBI, affirmed the finding that Wallace was not the victim of a hate crime but also stated that the rope should never have been fashioned into a noose *(NASCAR ARE PATHETIC PANDERERS)*. The organization committed to continuing its efforts to make the sport more inclusive and welcoming, acknowledging the incident as a learning experience in addressing issues of race and sensitivity.

Reflections on the Incident

The Bubba Wallace incident serves as a case study in how race, sports, and media intersect and influence public perception. It highlighted the challenges of addressing racism in high-profile settings and the potential for misunderstandings or misinterpretations in highly charged environments. The incident also underscored the importance of thorough investigation and the dangers of jumping to conclusions.

Legacy and Ongoing Discussions

While some argue that the incident was blown out of proportion, others believe it was a necessary catalyst for conversation and change in NASCAR and beyond. Wallace became an emblematic figure in the sport's journey toward greater diversity and inclusion. The incident, while not resulting in a hate crime charge, prompted NASCAR and its community to reflect on their practices and the signals they send about race and inclusivity.

Conclusion

The Bubba Wallace noose incident in NASCAR is a complex narrative that encapsulates the broader societal challenges of grappling with racism and prejudice. While the initial fears of a hate crime were debunked, the incident forced NASCAR and its fans to confront uncomfortable questions about race and the sport's culture. It demonstrated the rapid escalation and de-escalation of perceived racial incidents in the public eye and underscored the need for careful, nuanced approaches to sensitive racial and social issues. END

"HANDS UP, DON'T SHOOT"

Did you ever see the video of Michael Brown? Did you see him go into that market, steal, and cause a bunch of ruckus and then start traveling down the street unconcerned? Did you ever see his interaction with the police officer? That was on video as well.

A lot was on video concerning Michael Brown.

The video sources were out there to show you exactly how pretty much everything went down. And you know what you didn't see? You DID NOT see him (and I stress did not!) see him throw his hands up and say, "don't shoot".

The fact of the matter is that never happened!

But you were told in the media and everywhere else that it did happen!

That innocent baby Michael Brown went into a market to rob the place, innocently. Didn't cause any kind of a disturbance, innocently. Left the store, innocently. Was minding his own business as he walked down the street, innocently. Did not attack a police officer, innocently. Did not turn his back towards the police officer and walk away after attacking him, innocently. Did not turn back around towards the cop to attack the cop again, innocently.

No, what you heard was poor little Michael Brown, the 230lb 6ft something something black man who was completely innocent, was killed by a police officer while innocently saying, "hands up, don't shoot".

It was a great hoax for the left. It caused immeasurable damage to the nation. It did exactly what they wanted it to do.

This is what AI says about this hoax:

The phrase "Hands up, don't shoot" became emblematic of broader national discussions about police brutality and racial injustice in the United States, particularly after the shooting of Michael Brown in Ferguson, Missouri, on August 9, 2014. However, subsequent investigations revealed that the narrative surrounding the phrase did not fully align with the factual evidence of the event, leading to significant controversy and debate about the incident's portrayal and its aftermath.

Origin of the Incident

Michael Brown, an 18-year-old African American, was fatally shot by Darren Wilson, a white Ferguson police officer. The shooting occurred after a confrontation between Brown and Wilson, leading to widespread protests and civil unrest in Ferguson and across the country.

Emergence of the Phrase

The phrase "Hands up, don't shoot" originated from witness accounts claiming that Brown had his hands raised in surrender when he was shot by Officer Wilson. These accounts were widely circulated in the media and quickly became a rallying cry for protesters and activists who saw the shooting as a clear case of police brutality and systemic racial injustice.

Investigation and Findings

The U.S. Department of Justice (DOJ) conducted an extensive investigation into the shooting. In its report, released in March 2015, the DOJ found that the most credible evidence did not support the claim that Brown had his hands up in surrender when he was shot. Instead, the report concluded that the physical and forensic evidence, along with credible witness statements, supported the conclusion that Brown was moving toward Officer Wilson when he was shot.

Impact on Public Perception

The "Hands up, don't shoot" narrative had a profound impact on public perception, contributing to the national conversation about police use of force and racial disparities in law enforcement. It became a symbol of the Black Lives Matter movement and was used in protests and demonstrations across the country.

Controversy and Criticism

The revelation that the narrative might not be entirely accurate led to controversy and criticism. Some argued that the propagation of the "Hands up, don't shoot" narrative, despite conflicting evidence, exacerbated tensions between law enforcement and communities and contributed to a distorted perception of police actions.

Critics of the media and certain activists argued that the quick spread of an unverified narrative contributed to misunderstanding and misinformation surrounding the shooting. They contended that the narrative might have overshadowed the broader, legitimate concerns about police practices and racial injustice.

Broader Implications

The Ferguson incident and the "Hands up, don't shoot"
narrative had lasting implications for American society.
They sparked a nationwide discussion about race, justice,
and the way law enforcement interacts with communities,
particularly African American communities. The incident led
to calls for police reform, increased use of body cameras,
and greater scrutiny of police conduct.

Reevaluation and Reflection

Over time, as more details of the case emerged and were
analyzed, public discourse shifted to a broader examination
of systemic issues in policing and the criminal justice
system. While the specific claim that Brown had his hands
up in surrender when shot was widely challenged, the
phrase "Hands up, don't shoot" continued to be used as a
broader symbol of protest against police violence and racial
inequality.

Conclusion

The phrase "Hands up, don't shoot" and the shooting of
Michael Brown had a significant impact on the United
States, sparking national debates about policing, race, and
justice. While the specific circumstances of Brown's death
were more complex than initially portrayed, the phrase
encapsulated deep-seated feelings of injustice and mistrust

toward law enforcement in many communities. The legacy of Ferguson and the phrase "Hands up, don't shoot" continue to influence discussions about racial justice and policing in America. END

YASMIN SEWEID BREAKS CURFEW

The Yasmin Seweid hoax was a highly publicized incident that occurred in December 2016, during a period of heightened social and political tension in the United States following the election of Donald Trump. Seweid, a Muslim-American teenager from New York, initially claimed that she was attacked by three drunk white men on a New York City subway. According to Seweid, the men attempted to pull off her hijab while shouting pro-Trump slogans and making Islamophobic comments. This incident, as reported, quickly caught the attention of the media, police, and public due to its nature and the alleged motive behind the attack, which was directly linked to the inflammatory rhetoric associated with Donald Trump's presidential campaign.

The Initial Report

Yasmin Seweid reported to the police and subsequently told various media outlets that on the night of December 1, 2016, while traveling on the subway in Manhattan, she was harassed by three young white men. She claimed these men, who appeared intoxicated, yelled "Donald Trump!" along with other anti-Islamic slurs, and tried to snatch her hijab — a headscarf worn by some Muslim women. Seweid recounted that they called her a terrorist and shouted other derogatory terms linked to her Muslim identity.

The story rapidly gained traction on social media and was covered extensively by local and national news, reflecting the country's charged political and social atmosphere. The incident was held up as an example of the growing tide of hate crimes, which were reported to have spiked during and after the 2016 presidential election. Activists, community leaders, and ordinary citizens expressed outrage and solidarity with Seweid, seeing her reported ordeal as emblematic of the challenges faced by minority communities in the wake of Trump's election.

Investigation and Revelation

The New York City Police Department (NYPD) began an intensive investigation into the incident due to its seriousness and the public attention it garnered. Detectives reviewed surveillance footage from the subway system and nearby areas and interviewed potential witnesses. However, inconsistencies soon began to emerge in Seweid's account, and no corroborating evidence was found to back her claims.

Under further questioning, Seweid's story unraveled. Approximately two weeks after the incident, she admitted to fabricating the entire story. Seweid disclosed to the police that she had made up the attack to cover up for staying out late drinking with friends, which she feared would upset her strict Muslim parents.

Motivations Behind the Hoax

The motivations behind Seweid's false claim were rooted in personal issues rather than political activism. According to her statements to the police, she concocted the story to avoid punishment from her family for breaking curfew and for engaging in behaviors they disapproved of. However, the specifics of her claim — involving aggressive Trump supporters — tapped into the broader societal fears at the time, making her story instantly believable and resonant to many who were concerned about a surge in hate crimes.

Legal and Social Consequences

Following her admission, Yasmin Seweid was charged with filing a false police report and was later sentenced to community service after pleading guilty. The case stirred a considerable debate about the ramifications of false reporting, not only in terms of wasting police resources but also in terms of its impact on genuine victims of hate crimes. Critics argued that incidents like this could undermine the credibility of future claims of harassment and violence.

The public reaction to the revelation was mixed, with some expressing sympathy for Seweid's position, while others felt betrayed, emphasizing that false reports harm actual victims of hate crimes and could potentially fuel skepticism about legitimate incidents. The Muslim community, in particular, expressed concern about the potential backlash and the reinforcement of stereotypes about Muslims as untrustworthy.

Media Reflections and Lessons Learned

The media was also subject to scrutiny and criticism for its role in quickly amplifying unverified claims. The Seweid case served as a cautionary tale about the need for thorough vetting and fact-checking before reporting. It highlighted the challenges faced by journalists in an era where sensational stories, especially those involving hot-button issues like race, religion, and politics, are quickly spread and accepted.

Conclusion

The Yasmin Seweid hoax is a complex case that reflects broader societal issues. It serves as an example of how personal motivations can become intertwined with national political narratives, leading to significant public and media missteps. The incident underscores the importance of critical scrutiny of all allegations, particularly those that are charged with political and cultural significance. It also serves as a reminder of the human tendency to fit complex narratives into pre-existing beliefs, a dynamic that is especially potent in the realm of social and political discourse. END

THE RACIST AIR FORCE

The incident at the U.S. Air Force Academy Preparatory School in 2017, where racial slurs were initially reported to have been written on message boards outside the dorm rooms of five African American cadet candidates, sparked significant media attention and public discourse about racial intolerance within military institutions. However, the incident took an unexpected turn when it was revealed that one of the African American cadet candidates had fabricated the entire scenario. This revelation had broader implications for the Air Force Academy, affecting perceptions of military readiness and the institution's ability to foster a cohesive and inclusive environment.

Background of the Incident

In September 2017, the Air Force Academy Preparatory School found itself at the center of a racial controversy when derogatory slurs were reportedly found written outside the dormitory rooms of several Black cadet candidates. The discovery prompted immediate condemnation from military leadership and the public. Lt. Gen. Jay Silveria, then-Superintendent of the Air Force Academy, responded with a forceful speech that garnered national attention, emphasizing the importance of dignity and respect while telling racists to "get out" if they could not treat their peers appropriately. This speech was initially praised for its strong stance against racism and was widely shared across social media platforms and news outlets.

Investigation and Revelation

The Air Force Office of Special Investigations took charge of the case and began a thorough investigation into the racist messages. The inquiry eventually led to an unexpected conclusion: the investigation found that one of the supposed victims, an African American cadet candidate, had written the slurs himself. This cadet later admitted to fabricating the incident, although specific motives were not publicly disclosed.

Impact on Military Readiness and Cohesion

The revelation that the incident was a hoax had several immediate and long-term effects on the Air Force Academy and its perception of military readiness:

1. Trust and Cohesion: Military effectiveness relies heavily on trust and cohesion within the ranks. The hoax undermined these essential qualities, as cadets and staff grappled with the implications of such an act within their community. It prompted a reassessment of the trust cadets placed in one another and damaged the sense of camaraderie that military academies strive to build.
2. Leadership and Response: The incident tested the leadership skills of the Academy's top officials, who had to navigate the fallout from the hoax. While the initial response by Lt. Gen. Silveria was widely lauded, the subsequent revelation that the

incident was fabricated put the Academy's leadership in a difficult position, challenging their ability to maintain morale and manage the public and internal perception of the incident.

3. Training and Education: The hoax prompted discussions about the need for enhanced training and educational programs at the Academy focused on diversity, inclusion, and the proper handling of racial issues. There was a recognition that even fabricated incidents could indicate underlying tensions or problems that needed to be addressed through training and dialogue.

4. Reputation and Public Perception: The Air Force Academy, like any military institution, depends partly on public trust and support for its success and recruitment efforts. The incident and its aftermath negatively impacted the Academy's reputation, leading to concerns about its ability to attract and retain diverse talent. Restoring its image required significant effort and outreach to reassure the public and potential cadets of the Academy's commitment to integrity and diversity.

5. Policy Reevaluation: The event led to a reevaluation of policies regarding how such incidents are handled, investigated, and reported. Ensuring fairness in the investigative process and protecting the rights of all parties involved became a focal point for policy improvement.

Lessons Learned and Moving Forward

The Air Force Academy used this challenging situation as a learning opportunity, emphasizing the need for continuous dialogue on race relations and the importance of integrity within the cadet corps. The incident also highlighted the potential dangers of assuming facts before a thorough investigation is completed, teaching cadets and leaders alike the importance of patience and diligence in the face of sensitive issues.

Conclusion

While the hoax at the Air Force Academy Preparatory School was an isolated incident, its impact was felt across the military institution, affecting its readiness by challenging its internal cohesion, trust, and public image. The event served as a stark reminder of the complexities of managing race-related issues within a military context and underscored the need for robust mechanisms to foster an inclusive and respectful environment. It also demonstrated the resilience of military leadership in the face of unexpected challenges, reinforcing the importance of strong leadership in maintaining unit cohesion and readiness in any situation. END

"NOT ANOTHER RACIST NOTE!?"

In April 2017, St. Olaf College, a small liberal arts school in Minnesota, was thrust into the national spotlight after reports of a racist note left on a black student's car sparked significant campus protests and caught the attention of national media. The note included threatening, racist language and led to several days of student-led protests that culminated in a boycott of classes. The incident not only disrupted the academic schedule but also ignited intense discussions around race relations on campus and the administration's response to racial incidents.

Background of the Incident

The controversy began when Samantha Wells, an African-American student at St. Olaf College, reported finding a racist note on her car. The note contained an N-word and warned her to shut up or face consequences. Wells posted an image of the note on social media, which quickly spread across the campus and beyond, sparking outrage and condemnation. The content of the note was linked to broader national concerns about increasing racial tensions, often attributed to the polarizing 2016 presidential election.

The Campus Reaction

The discovery of the note led to a strong reaction from the St. Olaf student body. Students organized protests, demanding immediate action and response from the college administration to address what they saw as a campus climate that tolerated racism. The protests grew in intensity, leading to students boycotting classes and staging a sit-in at the school's cafeteria. They demanded that the administration implement new policies on racial tolerance and improve the support system for minority students.

Media Coverage

The incident received considerable attention from both local and national media outlets. News coverage highlighted the protests and the demands of the students, placing the incident within a larger narrative of racial issues at American colleges. Amidst a climate of heightened sensitivity to racial injustices and amidst several high-profile racial incidents on other campuses, the St. Olaf case was portrayed as part of a systemic problem facing institutions of higher education across the United States.

Media outlets covering the story provided a platform for voices from both within and outside the St. Olaf community, reflecting on the racial dynamics of not just St. Olaf College but the country as a whole. The coverage generally portrayed the student activists positively, focusing on their demands for a safer and more inclusive campus environment.

Investigation and Revelation

The college administration responded to the protests by initiating an investigation into the incident. However, the situation took a dramatic turn when it was later revealed that the supposed victim, Samantha Wells, admitted to creating the hoax herself. In emails to the student body, she stated that she fabricated the incident as a "strategy to draw attention to concerns about the campus climate."

This revelation prompted a complex secondary wave of reactions. The college administration faced criticism for its handling of the incident, particularly regarding how quickly they initially accepted the hoax as truth without sufficient investigation. Additionally, there was significant backlash from both the student body and the wider community, who felt betrayed and manipulated.

Impact of the Hoax

The uncovering of the hoax had a profound impact on St. Olaf College. It prompted a broader discussion about the authenticity of claims of racism and the potential backlash against legitimate cases of racial abuse. For some, it undermined real experiences of racism, while for others, it highlighted the need for more careful and nuanced handling of such accusations.

The incident also sparked a dialogue about the implications of false reporting on racial incidents. It raised questions about the balance between swift action against racism and the need for thorough verification of claims before taking action. The fallout from the hoax was a cautionary tale for educational institutions on managing allegations of racism and the importance of fostering an environment where racial issues are addressed with both seriousness and careful scrutiny.

Conclusion

The St. Olaf College hoax serves as a significant case study in the dynamics of race, media, and politics in contemporary America. It underscores the complexities involved in addressing issues of race in an educational setting and the potential consequences of actions driven by good intentions but executed without thorough verification. The media's role in shaping the narrative around such incidents also highlights the power of coverage in influencing public perception and the importance of journalistic integrity. In the end, the St. Olaf incident leaves behind lessons about the need for balance in activism, media reporting, and administrative response in the sensitive arena of racial relations. END

"TAWANA?" "NO!"

The Tawana Brawley case, which erupted in 1987, remains one of the most controversial and widely discussed alleged hoaxes in the history of the United States. The case revolved around 15-year-old Tawana Brawley, who claimed she was abducted and raped by a group of white men. The incident inflamed existing racial tensions and became a media sensation, involving prominent figures in the civil rights community and leading to significant public debate over issues of race, justice, and media responsibility. This essay explores the unfolding of the Tawana Brawley case, the investigation findings, the media's role, and the long-term impact of the incident.

Background of the Incident

In November 1987, Tawana Brawley, an African American teenager from Wappingers Falls, New York, was found in a trash bag, smeared with feces, and with racist epithets written on her body. She was discovered in a semi-conscious state and taken to a hospital, where she told a story that shocked the nation. Brawley claimed that she had been abducted and repeatedly raped by a group of white men, some of whom, she alleged, were law enforcement officers.

Immediate Response and Media Frenzy

The allegations made by Brawley instantly captured the media's attention and ignited widespread outrage. Given the severity of the accusations and the racial dynamics involved, the case quickly gained national significance. Newspapers and television networks covered the story extensively, often framing it as a clear example of racial injustice and systemic racism in the United States.

The involvement of civil rights activists such as Al Sharpton, Alton Maddox, and C. Vernon Mason added further credibility to Brawley's claims in the public eye. These figures supported Brawley's accusations and used the case as a platform to address broader issues of racial discrimination and police brutality.

The Investigation

A grand jury was convened to investigate the claims made by Brawley. The investigation was comprehensive, involving numerous interviews and an extensive review of medical records and other evidence. As the inquiry progressed, significant discrepancies and inconsistencies in Brawley's story began to surface.

Medical examinations did not support the claim of sexual assault, and despite extensive probing, investigators found no forensic evidence to corroborate Brawley's allegations of abduction and rape. Moreover, witnesses and alibis contradicted the timeline and circumstances described by Brawley.

After seven months of investigation, the grand jury released a 170-page report which concluded that Brawley had not been abducted, assaulted, raped, or subjected to any racial attack as she had claimed. Instead, the report suggested that Brawley might have fabricated the story to avoid punishment from her family for staying out late.

Media Critique and Reactions

The revelation that the allegations might have been fabricated led to a significant backlash against both the media and the civil rights activists who had championed Brawley's cause. Critics argued that the media had been too eager to accept the story without sufficient scrutiny because it fit a particular narrative about race relations in America.

The media's role in amplifying the story without adequate verification was widely criticized, raising serious questions about journalistic ethics and responsibilities. The case served as a cautionary tale about the potential dangers of sensationalist reporting, particularly in cases involving sensitive issues of race and violence.

Legal and Social Aftermath

The legal and social aftermath of the Brawley case was complex. Steven Pagones, an assistant district attorney whom Brawley had accused of being one of her assailants, sued Brawley, Sharpton, Maddox, and Mason for defamation. In 1998, a jury found that the defendants had defamed Pagones, awarding him a substantial sum in damages.

The Brawley case had lasting impacts on the individuals involved and prompted wider reflections on race, justice, and the role of the media in shaping public perceptions. For many, the case underscored the need for caution and rigor in addressing allegations of racially motivated crimes.

Reflections on Racial Tensions and Justice

The Tawana Brawley case remains a pivotal event in discussions about race and justice in America. It highlights the complexities of addressing allegations of racial violence and the challenges posed by media coverage of such sensitive issues. The case is often cited in debates about the presumption of innocence, the impact of race on perceptions of guilt and victimhood, and the responsibilities of public figures in advocating for justice.

Conclusion

The Tawana Brawley hoax is a deeply instructive episode that highlights the intersections of race, media, and justice. It serves as a reminder of the potential consequences of unchecked media sensationalism and the importance of a cautious and balanced approach to sensitive racial and legal issues. As such, the Brawley case continues to be studied and referenced in discussions about civil rights, media ethics, and the dynamics of race in America, underscoring its enduring relevance and the lessons it holds for journalists, activists, and policymakers alike. END

THE COVINGTON KIDS

If there's one thing the left likes to do it's accuse the other side of that which they are doing themselves. This is really part of the Communist Manifesto and it's one of the greatest tactics in the entire universe for them to use - because they know there are gullible and susceptible people that will fall for these type of hoaxes. Most of those people watch the news. And if they're not watching the news, they're definitely watching shows like The View.

So it wasn't a stretch to imagine that some kids at Covington got in trouble at a "protest" event which was staged by the Democrats. This protest didn't exist to make the kids look bad - and in fact, I dare you to even remember what the protest was about. You probably can't. (As I type this now, I have no idea). Even still, the press being the press, needed to "spread the word", and what better way than a bunch of MAGA loving kids minding their own business - just seeing what was happening.

What we saw on the news was a kid staring down this older Indian American - this Chief looking person - beating his drums and "standing for what he believed in". And for the press, that's an opportunity. Here's this young snot-nosed punk kid staring him down with a gratuitous smile on his face as if to say, "bring it on old man, bring it on."? We'll get him!

Now we know (because the truth doesn't always stay hidden) this "Chief" agitator (what today we call a troll), came up to *him* taunting and beating on his drums and got in the kids face. Pathetic.

We all saw that *after the hoax played its role* for the Democrat machine and the media. People believed it. Still believe it.

And the world bought into it because that was the media narrative. It wasn't true!

It was never true.

The Indian happens to have been a "professional agitator" and knew exactly what he was doing. And the press did too.

AI explains:

130

The Covington Catholic High School incident in January 2019 became a flashpoint in the national conversation about media bias, misinformation, and the power of social media to shape narratives. The incident involved students from Covington Catholic High School in Kentucky and Native American activist Nathan Phillips at the Lincoln Memorial in Washington, D.C.

The Incident

The initial media reports suggested that the students, many wearing "Make America Great Again" hats, had surrounded and taunted Phillips, who was participating in the Indigenous Peoples March. A short video clip appeared to show one of the students, Nick Sandmann, smirking at Phillips as he stood close to him, beating his drum. This clip went viral, leading to widespread condemnation of the students' alleged behavior.

The Broader Context

As longer videos of the incident emerged, the narrative began to shift. These videos showed that the students were not the instigators of the confrontation. Before Phillips approached them, the students were reportedly subjected to provocative and offensive taunts from a separate group, the Black Hebrew Israelites. Phillips then walked into the crowd of Covington students, beating his drum and chanting. The students, unsure of what was happening, reacted with confusion and nervous laughter. Sandmann, in particular, stood still and smiled, which he later described as an attempt to show he wanted no confrontation.

Media Backlash and Reevaluation

The initial portrayal of the incident led to significant backlash against the Covington students, particularly against Sandmann, who became the face of the incident due to his prominent position in the video. However, as the fuller context became known, many media outlets and individuals reevaluated their initial judgments. Critics accused the media of rushing to judgment and promoting a narrative that fit preconceived notions about race, politics, and privilege without a full understanding of the facts.

Impact on Nick Sandmann and Legal Actions

The incident had a profound impact on Nick Sandmann and the other Covington students. Sandmann received death threats and was subjected to intense public scrutiny and criticism. In response to what he and his family viewed as defamatory coverage, Sandmann filed defamation lawsuits against several major news organizations, including CNN and The Washington Post. These lawsuits were settled out of court, with the terms of the settlements undisclosed, though the settlements were viewed by some as an acknowledgment of unfair and damaging coverage.

The National Dialogue

The Covington Catholic incident sparked national debate over several issues, including the role of social media in spreading misinformation, the responsibilities of the press in verifying stories before publication, and the dangers of doxing and harassment. It also highlighted the polarized nature of American society, where individuals and events are often quickly slotted into existing political and cultural narratives.

Reflections and Lessons

The Covington incident serves as a cautionary tale about the rush to judgment and the power of initial impressions in the digital age. It underscored the importance of context in understanding events and the need for careful, nuanced reporting, especially in situations involving potential cultural or political flashpoints. The incident encouraged some media outlets and individuals to reflect on their practices and the impact of their words and coverage on real people's lives.

Conclusion

The Covington Catholic High School incident, centered

around the encounter between the students and Nathan
Phillips, remains a contentious and instructive episode in
the interplay between media, politics, and public perception.
While it exposed the pitfalls of rapid, context-free news
consumption and dissemination, it also provided an
opportunity for society to reflect on the complexities of
communication and judgment in the digital age. The
experiences of the main figures involved, especially Nick
Sandmann, highlight the personal and legal ramifications of
such media-driven events. END

THE RITTENHOUSE AFFAIR

Nothing would please those who are guarded by guns more than to get rid of guns for the rest of those that need guns to protect themselves.

To put it another way, the people who want to get rid of guns are always the people who are protected by armed security guards and guns.

So it was no surprise that they wanted to use the Kyle Rittenhouse episode in order to get rid of guns, once again.

You're probably familiar with this story because you've seen it on national news for years.

There was a 17 year old that went to protect businesses in a state, a town, an area, that he didn't live in but only a few miles away. As a result of him being there providing protection to these businesses, he was attacked and he defended himself. He ended up killing two people in defense of his own life - and he shot and injured a third person.

There was a huge trial where he was charged with numerous counts of murder and other things. But at the end of the day, the trial, though it did end well for Kyle and the rest of America who believes in the defense of businesses, homes, people, and children, did cause the media and the politicians to once again go crazy about gun control.

If killing babies is not the number one goal of Democrat and leftist politicians (and I mean killing babies in the womb), would their number one issue be to remove guns from American society so that they can simply kill you? Yes.

This effort to scapegoat Kyle, a 17-year-old kid trying to protect businesses, families, and other people was nothing more than an attempt by the media and the Democrats to pass quick legislation. "Oh look we've got to pass this gun law now".

Because everything they do comes with a plan. Everything you read about in this book, all the hoaxes, come with a plan. And if there is no plan they will make a plan up as they go along. And typically the plan is always about limiting your rights to your freedom and subverting the Constitution.

According to AI:

The Kyle Rittenhouse case became one of the most polarizing and heavily scrutinized legal battles in recent American history, unfolding against the backdrop of nationwide protests over police brutality and racial injustice. The incident, which took place in Kenosha, Wisconsin, during protests following the shooting of Jacob Blake by a police officer, resulted in Rittenhouse shooting three people, killing two and wounding one. His trial and subsequent acquittal sparked intense debate over self-defense laws, the role of armed civilians in public protests, and media bias.

The Incident and Immediate Aftermath

On August 25, 2020, then-17-year-old Kyle Rittenhouse, armed with an AR-15 style rifle, joined other armed individuals in Kenosha with the stated intention of protecting businesses from rioting amid ongoing protests. During the night, Rittenhouse shot three individuals: Joseph Rosenbaum, Anthony Huber, and Gaige Grosskreutz, leading to the deaths of Rosenbaum and Huber.

Media Portrayal and Public Perception

The media's treatment of the Rittenhouse case was marked by controversy and accusations of bias from the outset. Initial reports often portrayed Rittenhouse as an active shooter or vigilante who had recklessly inserted himself into a volatile situation. Some media outlets emphasized his presence at a Black Lives Matter protest with a firearm, framing him as a counter-protester or aggressor. This narrative contributed to a widespread perception of Rittenhouse as a symbol of racially motivated violence and vigilantism.

Legal Proceedings and Defense Strategy

Rittenhouse faced multiple charges, including first-degree intentional homicide, first-degree reckless homicide, and attempted first-degree intentional homicide. His defense argued that he acted in self-defense, a claim supported by video evidence showing confrontations with the men he shot. The defense contended that Rittenhouse only fired his weapon after being attacked and that he had tried to retreat before being forced to use his gun.

Trial and Acquittal

During the trial, the prosecution faced challenges in countering the self-defense argument, particularly given video evidence and witness testimonies that corroborated

Rittenhouse's version of events. In November 2021, after a highly publicized and contentious trial, Rittenhouse was acquitted of all charges. The jury, apparently persuaded by the self-defense claim, concluded that he reasonably believed his life was in danger during the incidents.

Media Criticism and Factual Discrepancies

The acquittal led to intensified scrutiny of the media's role in shaping public perception of the case. Critics argued that early reporting failed to adequately consider evidence suggesting Rittenhouse acted in self-defense and that the narrative was often more aligned with broader political and social themes than with the specific facts of the case. The discrepancy between the initial media narrative and the trial evidence led to discussions about media responsibility, particularly in high-stakes legal cases with significant public interest.

Impact of the Case

The Rittenhouse case had far-reaching implications, touching on issues of gun rights, self-defense laws, the role of individuals in public protests, and media bias. The trial underscored the complexities of legal interpretations of self-defense, especially in chaotic and violent situations. Additionally, it raised questions about the presence of armed civilians at protests and their impact on public safety and order.

Reflection on Media and Legal Systems

The case highlighted concerns about pretrial publicity and its potential to influence public opinion and juror impartiality. It brought to the forefront the challenges faced by the legal system in conducting fair trials in the age of instant news and social media, where narratives can be quickly established and difficult to challenge.

Conclusion

The Kyle Rittenhouse shooting and trial exemplify the intersection of legal, social, and media dynamics in contemporary American society. The case revealed not only legal and ethical questions about self-defense and civil unrest but also broader issues regarding media coverage and its effects on public perception and justice. Rittenhouse's acquittal, seen by some as a vindication of self-defense rights and by others as a failure of the justice system, remains a contentious and defining moment that continues to evoke strong feelings and debate. END

DUKE LACROSSE R*PE

The Duke lacrosse case, which unfolded in 2006, remains one of the most infamous legal and media circuses in recent U.S. history. It involved false accusations of rape and sexual assault made against members of the Duke University men's lacrosse team, leading to a national debate on issues of race, privilege, and justice.

Initial Accusations

The case began in March 2006 when Crystal Mangum, an African American woman working as a stripper, dancer, and escort, accused three white members of the Duke University lacrosse team—Reade Seligmann, Collin Finnerty, and David Evans—of raping her at a party held by the team. These allegations immediately ignited a firestorm of media attention and public scrutiny.

Media Frenzy and Public Reaction

The media extensively covered the story, often framing it as a clear-cut case of privileged white athletes assaulting an African American woman. This narrative tapped into broader themes of racial inequality and class privilege, sparking widespread outrage and leading to public condemnations of the accused players and the broader lacrosse team culture. The Duke lacrosse team's season was canceled, and the coach resigned amid the escalating scandal.

Legal Proceedings

Mike Nifong, the Durham County District Attorney at the time, aggressively pursued the case, making numerous public statements affirming the strength of the evidence against the players. However, as the case progressed, significant issues with the prosecution's evidence and ethical questions about Nifong's conduct began to emerge.

The Case Unravels

By late 2006 and early 2007, the case against the Duke players began to fall apart. It was revealed that there was a lack of DNA evidence linking any of the accused to the alleged victim. The DNA found did not match any team member but instead matched multiple other men, none of whom were connected to the lacrosse team.

Further investigation showed that Nifong had withheld exculpatory DNA evidence from the defense and made numerous procedural and ethical violations. Additionally, critical inconsistencies in Mangum's account and a lack of corroborating evidence raised serious doubts about the veracity of the allegations.

Dismissal and Aftermath

In April 2007, the North Carolina Attorney General's office took over the case from Nifong and, after conducting its own comprehensive review, dismissed all charges against the three players, declaring them innocent of the accusations. The Attorney General criticized the handling of the case, stating that the accused were victims of a "tragic rush to accuse."

The fallout from the case was significant. Mike Nifong was disbarred for his misconduct in handling the investigation. The Duke players filed civil lawsuits against Nifong, the City of Durham, and Duke University, leading to undisclosed financial settlements.

Reflections on the Case

The Duke lacrosse case became a cautionary tale about the dangers of preconceived notions and bias in the justice system and media. It highlighted the potential for media narratives to influence legal proceedings and public opinion, often at the expense of due process and fairness.

The case also sparked discussions about the intersections of race, gender, and privilege in the United States, with many commentators reflecting on how these dynamics influenced both the public's and the media's response to the allegations.

Conclusion

The Duke lacrosse case remains a potent example of a legal and media narrative gone awry, where initial assumptions and biases led to a deeply flawed and unjust prosecution. It serves as a reminder of the importance of due process, the dangers of media sensationalism, and the need for careful, unbiased investigation. END

MICHIGAN "KIDNAPPING"

The case surrounding the alleged plot to kidnap Michigan Governor Gretchen Whitmer in 2020 is complex and multi-faceted, involving issues of domestic terrorism, entrapment, and the role of law enforcement informants. This event gained national attention and sparked discussions about political extremism and the tactics used by government agencies to thwart potential threats.

Background and Initial Arrests

In October 2020, the FBI announced that it had thwarted a plot by a group of men to kidnap Governor Gretchen Whitmer. The individuals involved were linked to militia groups, and their alleged plan was said to be motivated by opposition to Whitmer's COVID-19 policies, which they viewed as overly restrictive. Thirteen men were arrested and charged with various federal and state crimes, including kidnapping conspiracy and terrorism-related offenses.

The Role of Informants and Undercover Agents

As the case unfolded, it became clear that the FBI had infiltrated the group with informants and undercover agents early in the planning stages. These operatives played significant roles in the group's activities, leading to allegations that the plot's development was heavily influenced, or even instigated, by these government representatives.

Defense attorneys for the accused argued that their clients were entrapped, claiming that the informants and undercover agents actively encouraged the plot and helped to organize meetings, training sessions, and surveillance activities. This argument suggested that, without government intervention, the group might not have progressed to an actionable kidnapping plan.

Trial and Acquittal

The trials for the accused individuals brought mixed outcomes. Some were convicted on charges related to the plot, while others were acquitted, raising questions about the extent of the group's intentions and capabilities to carry out the kidnapping. The defense's entrapment argument gained traction in some cases, leading to acquittals and sparking debate about the line between preventing crime and provoking it.

Media Coverage and Public Perception

Media coverage of the plot and the subsequent trials was intense, with some outlets focusing on the potential for right-wing extremism and terrorism, while others emphasized the entrapment defense and the role of the FBI

in possibly overstepping its bounds. This coverage
influenced public perception of the case, with opinions often
divided along political lines.

Political and Legal Implications

The alleged kidnapping plot had significant political and
legal ramifications. It brought attention to the rise of militia
movements and domestic extremism in the United States,
and it raised concerns about the balance between
surveillance, security, and civil liberties. The case also had
implications for Governor Whitmer's public image and
political career, as she faced both increased sympathy from
supporters and heightened criticism from opponents.

Reflections on Law Enforcement Tactics

The Whitmer kidnapping plot case led to discussions about
the tactics used by law enforcement agencies to infiltrate
and disrupt extremist groups. Critics argued that the
operation bordered on entrapment, with government agents
playing too active a role in developing the plot. In contrast,
supporters of the operation maintained that the FBI's
actions were necessary to prevent a potential act of
domestic terrorism.

Conclusion

The alleged plot to kidnap Governor Gretchen Whitmer and

the subsequent legal battles highlight the challenges of addressing domestic extremism while safeguarding individual rights. The case's complexities, including the significant involvement of informants and undercover agents, the mixed trial outcomes, and the intense media attention, underscore the difficulties in distinguishing between real threats and those potentially exacerbated or even created by law enforcement actions. END

"WE'RE COMING FOR KAVANAUGH NOW"

The confirmation process for Brett Kavanaugh, nominated by President Donald Trump to the U.S. Supreme Court in July 2018, became one of the most contentious and controversial judicial proceedings in recent American history. It was marked by intense political struggle and allegations of past sexual assault that captured the nation's attention, sparking debates about character, truthfulness, and the standards to which Supreme Court nominees should be held.

Background and Nomination

Brett Kavanaugh was a well-known figure in conservative legal circles with an extensive career in law and government service. Prior to his nomination to the Supreme Court, he served as a judge on the U.S. Court of Appeals for the District of Columbia Circuit. His judicial record was scrutinized, but it was the accusations of sexual misconduct that dramatically shifted the focus and intensity of the hearings.

The Allegations

The allegations against Kavanaugh came to public attention when Dr. Christine Blasey Ford, a professor of psychology at Palo Alto University and a research psychologist at the Stanford University School of Medicine, came forward with claims that Kavanaugh had sexually assaulted her at a high school party in the early 1980s. According to Dr. Ford, Kavanaugh, then 17, pinned her to a bed, groped her, and attempted to remove her clothing while he was drunk at a party. Dr. Ford alleged that Kavanaugh's friend, Mark Judge, was also present in the room and that both were laughing during the incident. She stated that she was able to escape when Judge jumped on the bed, sending all three tumbling.

As the Senate Judiciary Committee prepared to vote on Kavanaugh's nomination, Dr. Ford's allegations prompted a reopening of the hearings. The situation became a flashpoint for national debates over sexual misconduct, victim rights, and due process.

The Hearings

In late September 2018, both Kavanaugh and Dr. Ford testified in a highly charged session before the Senate Judiciary Committee. Dr. Ford detailed her memories of the alleged assault, describing the events and their long-term impact on her life. She noted that the laughter of Kavanaugh and Judge during the assault was a poignant memory that had haunted her for decades.

Kavanaugh vehemently denied the allegations in an emotional testimony, asserting that he had never assaulted Dr. Ford or anyone else. He argued that the allegations were politically motivated and aimed at derailing his confirmation. Kavanaugh's forceful denial included expressions of frustration with the political process and the way the allegations were handled.

Public and Political Reactions

The nation was deeply divided in its response. Supporters of Kavanaugh saw the allegations as unsubstantiated and an unfair attack on his character and family, potentially based on mistaken identity or political bias. Critics believed Dr. Ford's testimony and felt that the allegations, if true, were disqualifying for a Supreme Court justice.

The hearings also reignited discussions about the treatment of sexual assault victims, the handling of such allegations from decades ago, and the appropriate level of scrutiny for public figures. The #MeToo movement, which had gained significant traction the year before, framed much of the public discourse, highlighting a societal shift towards taking allegations of sexual misconduct more seriously.

FBI Investigation and Senate Vote

Amidst public pressure, an additional FBI investigation was conducted into the allegations against Kavanaugh. The investigation was limited in scope and time, and its findings were not publicly disclosed in full, but it was reported to have found no corroboration for the allegations of sexual assault.

In early October 2018, after a heated debate, the Senate confirmed Kavanaugh to the Supreme Court by a narrow margin of 50-48, one of the closest votes in the history of Supreme Court confirmations. The vote reflected deep partisan divisions, with most Republicans supporting Kavanaugh and most Democrats opposing him.

Aftermath and Continuing Impact

The Kavanaugh hearings left a lasting impact on American politics and society. They not only influenced public trust in the Supreme Court but also affected how sexual assault allegations are perceived and handled in politically sensitive environments. For many, the hearings were seen as a critical moment that either reaffirmed or undermined the notion of judicial impartiality and integrity.

Moreover, the Kavanaugh confirmation battle underscored the increasingly partisan nature of Supreme Court nominations, suggesting that future confirmations might similarly be fraught with political conflicts and personal allegations. END

"BUT FIRST WE HAVE TO GET THOMAS"

The confirmation hearings of Clarence Thomas in 1991 to the U.S. Supreme Court were among the most controversial and closely watched in American history. The proceedings were thrust into the national spotlight primarily due to allegations of sexual harassment made by Anita Hill, a law professor who had previously worked under Thomas at the Department of Education and the Equal Employment Opportunity Commission (EEOC). The hearings, which initially focused on Thomas's legal philosophy and qualifications, were transformed into a broader cultural debate about sexual harassment in the workplace and gender dynamics in high-stakes political vetting processes.

Background of Clarence Thomas

Before his nomination to the Supreme Court by President George H.W. Bush, Clarence Thomas had built a career in various governmental legal positions. Known for his conservative views, particularly his skepticism toward affirmative action, which he himself had benefited from, Thomas was seen as a strong conservative choice to succeed Thurgood Marshall, the first African-American Supreme Court Justice. His nomination was initially contentious due to his judicial philosophy but became explosive with the emergence of Anita Hill's allegations.

Anita Hill's Allegations

Anita Hill, who had worked under Clarence Thomas at two federal agencies, came forward with allegations that Thomas had made inappropriate sexual remarks and advances toward her during their professional relationship. Hill's detailed testimony included descriptions of Thomas discussing explicit sexual material and making unwanted personal advances. Her calm and detailed testimony was broadcast live and watched by millions of Americans, highlighting issues of sexual harassment to an unprecedented degree.

Clarence Thomas's Response

Clarence Thomas vehemently denied the allegations, asserting that he was the victim of a "high-tech lynching for uppity blacks who in any way deign to think for themselves." His forceful denial was aimed not only at clearing his name but also at highlighting the racial dynamics at play, given that both he and Hill are African American. Thomas argued that the confirmation process had degenerated into a spectacle that undermined his dignity and integrity based on unproven allegations.

Public and Political Reaction

The hearings polarized public opinion and became a cultural watershed. Supporters of Thomas saw the allegations as unproven and a last-minute smear to derail the nomination of a conservative African American who did not align with the predominantly liberal civil rights agenda. Meanwhile, Hill's supporters saw her as a courageous figure standing up to a powerful man in a setting that was stacked against her. They argued that her detailed accounts of Thomas's behavior were credible and disqualifying for a lifetime appointment to the highest court in the land.

The Role of the Senate Judiciary Committee

The Senate Judiciary Committee, then chaired by Senator Joe Biden, faced criticism for its handling of the hearings. Critics argued that the all-male committee was not adequately prepared to handle allegations of sexual harassment and that Hill was subjected to aggressive questioning that sought to undermine her character and credibility. The committee's handling of the hearings is often cited as a case study in the failures of gender sensitivity and procedural justice in highly charged political environments.

Confirmation and Its Aftermath

Despite the controversy, the Senate narrowly confirmed

Clarence Thomas to the Supreme Court by a vote of 52-48, one of the closest confirmation votes in history. The hearings had a lasting impact on American politics and society, significantly raising public awareness and dialogue about sexual harassment in the workplace.

The hearings also had a measurable impact on subsequent political and judicial processes, contributing to what was called "The Year of the Woman" in 1992, during which a significant number of women were elected to Congress. The Thomas confirmation also influenced how future allegations of personal misconduct would be handled in political vettings and contributed to the development of more robust workplace policies against sexual harassment.

Legacy

The Clarence Thomas confirmation hearings remain a pivotal moment in U.S. political and social history, often revisited in discussions about judicial nominations, race, gender, and power dynamics in American public life. They underscore the complex interplay between personal conduct allegations and public vetting processes in the highest echelons of government. The hearings not only shaped the Supreme Court's composition but also transformed public consciousness and legislative approaches to sexual harassment, leaving a legacy that resonates in contemporary political discourse and policy making. END

"WOKE" IS A HOAX!

Perhaps the biggest hoax of all at this moment in history is that of the "WOKE" agenda.

What is the woke agenda? And what is 'woke'?

There was a time where people were ridiculed for not knowing the answer. Books were written. Videos were shot. Thousands of tweets were created "defining" woke.

Everyone got it wrong. Here's the real definition:

Woke is the Top-Down system people in power put in place in order to depopulate.

How you ask? I'm glad you asked. Let's start from the beginning:

PART 1 – HOW DID THIS ALL START?

The growth of simply being 'rebellious' in the 50's to where we find ourselves in the early 2020's is both amazing and terrifying.

I was thinking about how we went from 'rebellious' to 'enlightened' to 'progressive' to 'liberal' to now 'WOKE'. It isn't pretty, but there is a very clear thread combining each moment in history.

Almost everyone that became 'enlightened', started with being rebellious.

They had a family unit. Parents. A mother and a father. And more often back then, the parents weren't divorced.

In the early 1950's there was some semblance of family cohesion. Adults were still adults - and at least, partially respected.

But the nuclear family began to be broken up. The children born in the 1930's, who missed going into World War 2, realized in the 50's that less than a decade earlier, kids their current age were eager to sign up and fight.

159

Soon after in the 60's (largely because of the Vietnam War) these same rebellious kids became enlightened and took the "enlightened" thing to heart.

All of the sudden, they were smarter, brighter, more knowledgeable (3 things that mean the same thing) than anyone else; if only in their own mind. But after several years, being enlightened just wasn't enough any more.

Then the progressive wave came.

As mentioned earlier in the book, writers like Paul Ehrlich came out claiming that there were too many people in the world (without actually doing much about it himself). Much to the detriment of human society, "Dr." Fauci and Bill Gates took this message to heart (more on that later).

Ehrlich was an enlightened person, it seems. As an enlightened person, he had all the answers. With all the answers, the next logical step was to become a progressive - someone not only with all the answer, but with 'forward' thought on how we as a society should do things.

Progressive.

He wrote that book "The Population Bomb" that extolled the virtue of limiting the population to only himself and those that agreed with him. His thesis? The world needed less people, not more. And not surprisingly, many did agree with him. The book clearly made them feel special and set apart from the rest of the population (much in the same way Hitler's Mein Kompf did certain Germans).

In fact many continue to both agree and work to see Ehrlich's dream become a reality. These people are called "woke".

How did he become the darling superstar of death culture - and thus WOKE culture?

Traumatized from years of enlightened "thought" (after the Vietnam war), Universities were so afraid of teenagers, they gave him a position of power.

The media, not considering thousands of people just died in the war - and needing a new 'outrage' - gave him a platform. What's better to talk about on TV than having too many people on the planet? Seems outrageous we have to live with so many people - and how will we feed ourselves?!

And the progressive politicians, those that learned early how to divide and conquer a population, couldn't resist. They were going to trumpet that 'progressive' idea. Especially that idea.

A rebellious person doesn't know anything. An enlightened person knows everything. A progressive is an enlightened person who also knows what everyone should do about what they know. A liberal (politician) is the one who carries out the plan the progressive has. A 'woke' person falls for their own destruction. Depopulation.

Literally taking Ehrlich's advice to heart, Teddy Kennedy took it upon himself the lower the population - if only by one person. The senator from Massachusetts drunk drove his car into a canal and killed a woman in the process.

Nothing happened to him, and in fact the great people of Massachusetts continued to vote for him, election after election, until he ultimately ran for President of the United States.

162

He was a hero of the woke liberals (much like Che Guevara, who literally murdered woke people all the time, but still finds room on their t-shirts), up until the day he himself died.

PART 2 – THE DIVISION PLAN

The progressives and liberals looked forward. And started reshaping the world in the image they wanted it to be. It wouldn't come without resistance, but each time they met new resistance, a new type of 'crisis' would be introduced. And if it wasn't a crisis, it was a new way to divide people - which would of course, create a crisis.

The same way they destroyed the nuclear family, would be the same way they destroyed the rest of society, and maintain a tighter grip on power.

They sowed division in every way possible and separated people based on race, religion, and gender.

No longer were you a part of a large population, you were

relegated to a tiny subset of a subset. Which led to an even smaller subset. Which led to many people simply feeling 'they were alone'.

Before this, when you may have identified with a large group, now it was a personal choice to forgo societal norms and choose to be whatever you wanted to be.

It's not a coincidence that it was at this same time new pharmaceutical drugs were introduced at a phenomenal rate.

Ehrlich ultimately got it wrong, and in fact, continues to get it wrong. We didn't starve to death because we had too many people to feed. In fact, a guy came around and invented a new type of wheat which 'saved' millions of people around the world. His name was Norman Borlaug, and he won the Nobel Peace Prize as a result.

Years later Barack Obama would win the Nobel Peace Prize for ... well, no one is sure really. He became president and within no time and no achievements in office, won the award.

PART 3 – REBELLION!

WW1 gave way to the roaring 20's. The roaring 20's gave way to the Great Depression of the 30's. It wasn't until the 40's, and WW2, that things truly began to change.

Babies born in the Great Depression weren't old enough to go to war in the 40's, but by the late 40's and entering into the 50's, they had seen, and learned enough to know - the men and women fighting 'the Great War', were approximately their own age.

What's a person of that age supposed to do? ... 16, 17, 18 ... well, in the 1950's they chose to say, "men and women my age were fighting in a war only a few years ago, you can't tell me what to do!". And so they did.

Rebellion was born.

It was a fight against authority and those that told them

what they could, and should, do. How ironic that by one decade later, enlightenment would take hold and those born in the 1940's would soon be burning their draft card because the leaders they loved so much would get us entangled in yet another war (on a hoax btw! Tonkin didn't happen).

The rebellious would be enlightened, and turn to progressive, and then to liberal - and it was the very same liberals who sought to control the world. And have pretty much ever since (we're in a war now with Russia).

The same rebellious people of the 50's, who fought their parents and authority, who fought the draft in the 60's, who fought the establishment in the 70's literally became the establishment - and turned out to be 1,000 times worse than even the worst person of the 20's, 30's, 40's, or 50's.

Today, because of these same people, we live in a real time Animal Farm.

PART 4 – LOSING THE WAR OF ATTRITION

What happened? A series of conflicts. A series of battles. A

166

series of wars. With the biggest being a war of attrition. When good people laid down and said, "I give". There's no fighting it. It's coming whether I do anything about it or not.

Let's look at two "world leaders" as an example:

"Dr." Fauci, allegedly, primarily and ostensibly the man who helped create and release a deadly illegal gain of function research project funded by American tax payers into the world, took to heart what Ehrlich's book and entire message says, 'there are too many people on the planet and we have to do something about it'.

He sure did.

When testifying years earlier in front of Congress he essentially said that "something like a virus will escape from a lab somewhere and kill a population"; he was signaling his woke and authoritarian friends on the left that the time was getting nearer.

There is no irony in Bill Gates' 2010 address to the woke TED conference (the same one mentioned earlier in the book) where he basically said, "of all the things I could do to help {the world}, I could create a vaccine, which is something I love...".

Whether Fauci said what he said first, or Gates said what he said first, makes no difference. The two men were clearly signaling.

Fauci saying, "yes, this is coming"; Gates saying, "right behind you ole' pal".

We now know multi-millions of COVID deaths happened all over the world. And we are also beginning to realize why people like Gates 'love vaccines'.

They kill too.

And the worst is yet to come.

We already know that women's menstrual cycles have been disrupted - we just don't know to what degree. Will most child bearing aged women become sterile? Will newborns be deformed? Will women who took the vaccine, who are scared to even have children because of all the medical side affects, simply chose to not have children? Remains to be seen.

If your goal was to lower the population as Gates has said over and over, this would be a good way to do it.

And remember, this was 'born' in the 70's - the age of 'progressive' thought.

If we know anything, we know these people are willing to wait as long as it takes in their war of attrition.

By the time COVID did hit, it wasn't too hard to lock-down a country. Just do what the Chinese do! Just do it how they did it. Mask up. Stay in. Don't go to church. Don't see a family member in the hospital. Don't gather with friends. Take the damn vaccine! And the booster. And the booster's booster.

There was little rebellion. And those that did rebel were 'locked up, or out' of their voice. Twitter, YouTube, META / Facebook and countless other places caved to the pressure of someone voicing a concern or opinion. Even if they themselves were a doctor and had an informed opinion.

PART 5 – VAXX AND WAR

You think it's scary when you're watching a sporting event and a perfectly healthy 20-something player suddenly drops dead? Wait until you see perfectly healthy 20-something soldiers in battle suddenly dropping dead. And not from enemy fire but because they're running, ducking, covering, and their heart is racing and beating out of their chest.

Here comes the vaccine!

There simply hasn't been enough wars lately to be honest. Not enough to depopulate the Earth in the way the woke want the earth depopulated.

And wars, whether Republican or Democrat, are mostly never fought with any other intent other than to depopulate the earth.

That's why the world is headed into yet another world war.

170

There's simply too many people for these people.

As you recall, there are several common threads between rebellion, enlightened, progressive, liberal, and WOKE, with depopulation being one of the biggest.

If Fauci messed COVID up, and allegedly "accidentally" released a milder strain that didn't nearly have the killing effect he and others in the CDC and WHO hoped - and Gates' vaccine "cleanup" operation is working, but not nearly well enough as either hoped, then war is deemed necessary.

That goes double for the war on warriors. Why else would the military mandate a killer vaccine where companies releasing it can't be sued or held liable in any way?

Oh wait, the military is now woke too.

Combined with the World War every woke politician is working so hard to get us into (which may also go nuclear), you see all these years later the woke are still working on lowering the population.

PART 6 – VAXX AND ABORTION

Because of the vaccine, birth rates across the world in vaccinated countries are almost certain to hit a wall. As mentioned, we're already learning that the vaccine is messing up female menstrual cycles. *Wait until they find out what it can do to a baby in the womb.*

And that seems like part of the plan - especially now that Roe v. Wade has been overturned and punted back to the states.

Woke states will continue down their path of depopulation by passing laws ensuring "a woman's right to choose" (Minnesota already has). Some of these woke states may even go so far as former Gov. Northam wanted to go - which is infanticide - ie. killing a baby born alive, moments after it's birth (yes, these sick people want this).

But no matter, *young women of birthing age that have taken the vaccine and boosters, may not even have the opportunity to make their own "reproductive health decisions",* as it's more and more likely, that decision was made for them - either by government mandate, work mandate, or the psychological mandate - that of the bully pressure from others to "just get the damn shot!" as Biden said.

Whether it's what the vaccine does to the expectant baby (which we don't yet know), or what it's already done to the fertile mother (from brain to heart), birth rates are likely to decline.

Abortion did a great job, and they were so proud of it - and themselves. And don't get it wrong, abortion will continue, these people play the 'long game' - so it's not over, it's just punted.

Being the great defensive players that they are, they've ensured something that could be even more devastating to birth rates with this shot and it's endless boosters.

All part of the plan.

But there's also another plan that's been hatched, that if it continues, threatens to take birth rates down even further - all to the relief of the woke depopulation crowd.

LGBTQ+ etc.

PART 7 – LGBTQIA+etc.

If we do find that birthing aged women who got the vaccine and booster shots are less likely to be able to give birth, this will obviously make the woke crowd happy. But there's something else being foisted onto children that could really do some 'population damage' as well - *and that's the whole point of LGBTQ+etc.*

Hospitals like John Hopkins and Vanderbilt are chopping up children like zucchini.

"We'll take away little Sally's ability to have children by chopping her up. We'll take Johnny's ability to have children by chopping him up. See? Everyone wins!"

The more the genders, the more the sexual preferences, the more the 'fluidity' of individuals, the less chance humans will be created and born.

Already serious medical professionals in the presidential cabinet tell us, under oath in Congress, "men can menstruate".

Men, on the other hand, cannot menstruate.

If these men continue to choose to be with other men, or women with other women – and boys become gils and girls boys, what happens to the population? Naturally it will drop.

It's no secret why the push for woke gender studies and woke equity in colleges.

These institutions are teaching a much younger generation in their 20's, who will soon be teachers themselves, how to capture and indoctrinate the mind of children.

We already see this with "Drag Night at the Library" and "Family Friendly Drag Shows" which hold no semblance to anything remotely family friendly - with someone up on stage rubbing their genitalia and getting small kids to put money in their jock strap.

Children's books depicting graphic sexual encounters along the LGBTQ+etc lines are already populating even the youngest child's library in woke schools - and being 'approved' by woke school boards making decisions for children that a parent should be making.

Parents are on the defense, once again.

These woke people know that *in order to capture children as an adult, they have to capture them as a kid* - at the youngest age - it's called "grooming" for a reason.

Indeed there is a huge push in the woke academia (and media) to ensure the 'normalization' of something I won't even put on these pages - but suffice to say, it involves grown-ups and children in the most lurid way. You know what I'm talking about.

Sick people.

Here's the thing. These woke groomers, and indeed the entire LGBTQ+etc crowd will never have children themselves (ostensibly). They are sacrificing themselves for the 'greater good' of woke depopulation – and they don't even know it.

Now all they have to do is capture the children and teach them that it's 'okay' to 'be like them' (where else better to do this than the classroom, away from a parent?) - and within a few generations of this, the population, already wrecked by abortion, war, man made viruses that 'escaped' from a lab, vaccines and booster shots, and women unable to give birth, will decline significantly.

Being WOKE, from any angle it's looked at, and no matter what it is, can literally and every time be traced back to depopulation.

So what comes next?

PART 8 – WHAT NOW?

Where do we go from here?

177

Well, the rebellion of the 1950's shrank as enlightenment came on the scene in the 1960's. By the time Ehrlich proposed there were too many people on earth, the world had morphed into progressivism. Liberals soon followed the progressives and from there, WOKE was born.

Where we go from here is back to rebellion.

You can already see the signs of it as parents begin to fight back against woke indoctrination at schools. Some government officials are beginning to fight back on a state level in colleges. Some business leaders are fighting back against woke DEI and ESG investing.

Here's the problem. After a multi-decade war of attrition, the woke know how to play the long game. Give an inch, they take a mile.

From the time of rebellion to woke is some 70 YEARS of just taking inches. It's been a war of attrition. Where worn down by it all, normal people became - well, worn out.

"Okay, it's going to happen anyhow, just let it"

Inch after inch after inch.

Things never heard of in the whole of human history suddenly have become headline news. Accepted to a large degree. Overnight.

It won't end because the woke won't end. They will keep pushing. They will keep fighting this war of attrition with literally NO ending.

First it's 'accept this'. "Okay, as a decent society, we'll accept that." "Now accept this." Several years later, "Okay, as a decent society, we'll accept that too."

Fast forward 70 years of this and you have woke people, who have worn down decent people, telling them "ACCEPT THIS MASK, STAY IN YOUR HOUSE, DON'T GO TO CHURCH, DON'T MEET WITH FRIENDS, AND TAKE THE DAMN JAB!!" - and don't realize it's all about depopulation.

And decent people say, "Okay, if only to help everyone else."

But rebellion is coming. A new rebellion.

First people have to know, (and I know, I repeat myself) WOKE is the culture of death. Depopulation. Nothing else matters and there is only one battle being waged. It's to lower earth's population to the point the only people left are 'them' - and then they'll battle each other because there will be nothing left and only bugs to eat.

As soon as you realize what woke really is, you can begin to learn how to 'fight back' - and here's the real key to knowing how:

Enlightenment, progressive, liberal, woke - they've all grown up with the idea of "personal choice", but not personal responsibility.

PART 9 – PERSONAL CHOICE

Imagine growing up in a world where you have personal choice, but no personal responsibility.

That's the world the woke live in.

It's their choice to discard their unborn baby, but not their responsibility to have that baby and raise them into a productive member of society.

It's their choice to change from a man to a woman and back again, but not their responsibility to respect others who don't, and won't agree with what they are doing.

It's their choice to use a women's bathroom, where your young daughter may be, but not their responsibility to keep your young daughter from seeing their genitalia.

It's their choice to start a war in which hundreds of thousands of people can die, but not their responsibility to fight in it.

It's their choice to build a deadly gain of function virus and release it on the world, but not their responsibility to take responsibility for doing it.

It's their choice to open the border to illegal migrants

smuggling in fentanyl that literally kills tens of thousands of people each month, but not their responsibility to close the border and stop it from happening.

It's their choice to champion de-fund the police while knowing that with less police on the streets, more people will die - but not their responsibility to have "that lawlessness" in their own neighborhood.

It's their choice to champion "global warming" and "climate change" causes, but not their responsibility to stop their own destruction of the climate .

You get the idea.

Being woke is all about death. It's all about depopulation. *From the days of Ehrlich in the 1970's until now, that's all they've ever cared about.*

They may do battle over things that seem non-applicable, but a deep dive into everything they do - anything they fight for - clearly shows what the real and true motive is. Killing people. Or, put another way, ensuring a population that shrinks over time.

182

Fauci believes in it. Gates believes in it. The CDC and WHO believes in it. The world economic forum (who are actually very honest about it and just comes out and says what they believe) believes in it. The United Nations believes in it. Most governments around the world believe in it.

It's ALL a HOAX.

The only way to rebel, the only way to 'fight back', the only way to win is to push for a return to *personal responsibility*.

PART 10 – PERSONAL RESPONSIBILITY

When you think about personal responsibility (and let's caveat that - making clear we're talking to rational individuals like yourself) you think, "this person answers for their actions in a way that makes the world a better place."

To recap:

We spelled out what woke was - how the only thing the

woke truly are concerned with is depopulation.

Many may not even realize it. They've been sold this idea of 'personal choice' and that has led to their religion - which, when you boil it down, is nothing more than a culture of death.

Depopulation is a cult-like religion. It's name is woke.

Now let's talk about personal responsibility as a way to fight wokeness.

It's your responsibility to have the baby and raise them into a productive member of society - not a choice to simply discard it because "you feel like it".

It's your responsibility to remain the gender God gave you so that you can best serve humanity with that gender - not a choice as to which gender you "feel like".

It's your responsibility (as a man, or as a woman) to not use the restroom of the opposite gender, where young children could be - not your choice to show off your genitalia to these kids.

It's your responsibility to speak up when hundreds of thousands (if not millions) of illegal migrants (ie. likely 'drug mules') are coming over the border with no consequence and essentially invited to bring fentanyl killing drugs into the country - not your choice to simply watch the nightly news filled with all the homeless people dying from these drugs and say, 'oh well'.

It's your responsibility to seek a stronger, more active, and well funded police force in your community (actually 'fighting real crime' and not harassing normal people) - not sit back and wait for them to be de-funded and watch as crime skyrockets out of control.

You get the idea.

Your #1 responsibility is to fight the culture of death the woke bring to the table each and every hour, day, week, month, and year - and not lose the war of attrition they have fought for over 70 years - where you just throw your hands up, and give up.

HOAXSTERS, Inc.

How The Left Pushes False Narratives To Promote Division In America

Written by Paul King